GHOST STORIES
of PETS
and
ANIMALS

Darren

GHOST
HOUSE

Ghost House Books

The Publisher: Ghost House Books
Distributed by Lone Pine Publishing

10145 – 81 Avenue

Edmonton, AB T6E 1W9

Canada

1808 – B Street NW, Suite 140

Auburn, WA 98001

USA

Website: http://www.ghostbooks.net

National Library of Canada Cataloguing in Publication Data

Zenko, Darren, 1974–
  Ghost Stories of Pets and Animals / Darren Zenko.

  ISBN 1-894877-36-5

  1. Animal ghosts. I. Title.
BF1484.Z46 2003   133.1'4   C2003-911023-0

Editorial Director: Nancy Foulds
Project Editors: Chris Wangler, Scott Rollans
Illustrations Coordinator: Carol Woo
Production Coordinator: Gene Longson
Cover Design: Gerry Dotto
Layout & Production: Chia-Jung Chang

Photo Credits: Every effort has been made to accurately credit photographers. Any errors or omissions should be directed to the publisher for changes in future editions. The photographs and illustrations in this book are reproduced with the kind permission of the following sources: Istock (p. 8: H. Arsleasson; p. 11: Phil Singer; p. 44, 73: Diane Diederich; p. 69: L.K. Garrenson; p. 79: G. Goodfleisch; p. 81, 102: Alexei Nabarro; p. 84: Lukasz Chyrek; p. 93: Carlye Clark; p. 113: Eric Vessels); Library of Congress (p. 55: DIG-ppmsc-08678; p. 98: USZC4-2337; p. 101: USZ62-121528); Bill Hall (p. 87); Chia-Jung Chang (p. 104, 150, 174); Carol Woo (p. 195).

The stories, folklore and legends in this book are based on the author's collection of sources including individuals whose experiences have led them to believe they have encountered phenomena of some kind or another. They are meant to entertain, and neither the publisher nor the author claims these stories represent fact.

We acknowledge the financial support of the Government of Canada through the Book Publishing Industry Development Program (BPIDP) for our publishing activities.

PC: P5

*For Mom and Dad,
for everything*

Contents

Acknowledgments

First and foremost, thanks to editor Chris "Dawg" Wangler and publisher Shane Kennedy for their patience and support during the long and unexpectedly arduous process of this book's creation. Thanks also to illustrations coordinator Carol Woo, layout designer Chia-Jung Chang and the entire Ghost House team, a crackerjack squad of publishing ninjas you simply do not want to mess with.

Love and blessings to Shannon O'Toole for putting up with the madness of a stressed-out author, and likewise to my wonderful and caring parents and family, without whose support I'd probably be writing parole applications rather than spooky books. Cheers to Bob the Angry Flower creator Stephen Notley; "Fish" Griwkowsky; Dwayne Martineau; Jody Cloutier; the entire executive, staff and membership of the Mill Creek Storytellers' Society; Colleen Hope; and anyone anywhere who's ever cut me more slack than I probably deserved. I am literally indebted to you.

Thanks most of all to those who have told their tales, without whom this book could not possibly exist, and the entire community of ghost-story lovers and researchers whose efforts keep the legends alive. Thank you all. Keep sharing your stories!

Introduction

When this book was first discussed, there was a general agreement that the main theme would be the relationship between humans and animals, and how stories of ghost pets and animal apparitions illustrate that connection. It was to be primarily a collection of pet stories, accounts of Fidos and Fluffies whose spirits survive their physical passing.

As you'll see, it quickly became apparent that such stories make up only half, or even less than half, of the body of phantom-animal tales. For every beloved companion animal's spirit that still pads around its old home, there is a terrible dog at the crossroads, a weird creature in the walls, a beast in the woods. This is the other half of the human-animal equation; and as much as we may love our domesticated friends, and as much as they may love us back, animals still represent the unknown, the wilderness, the nonhuman forces of our dreams—and our nightmares.

Our folklore, the stories we tell, are part of who we are as people. They define us, and speak of our hopes and fears— in this case, the hope that our beloved companions might persist beyond physical life and physical death, and the fear that less friendly forces might enjoy the same privilege.

But in the end, after all the theory and psychology, these are stories, and their purpose is to entertain. Whether they're heartwarming or chilling, they're here to be enjoyed and shared. It's in this spirit of fun that this book was written, and it's in this spirit that I hope you will appreciate it. Thanks for reading; enjoy the trip.

1
History
and
Mystery

The Tower of Anguish

In nearly 1000 years of bloody history, the Tower of London has served as a military fortress, a jail, an execution ground and a place of torture. Of all the spooky places in the world, it's hard to imagine anywhere more appropriate for ghosts. The tower has seen enough death, despair and anguish to sustain a legion of grim specters—including at least one unusual animal ghost.

In 1078, a little more than a decade after his defeat of Harold at the Battle of Hastings, William the Conqueror chose the site for an imposing new fortress. The strategically valuable location, on the north bank of the Thames, was already the site of the ruins of a Roman fortification. One of the ancient walls, in good repair, was incorporated into the new building, which later became known as the White Tower.

Over the subsequent centuries, the site gradually grew into an 18-acre mass of walls, towers, chapels and houses. Today, the Tower of London houses England's Crown Jewels and attracts millions of tourists from all over the globe.

Though the tower's amazing architecture and living history provide the main draw—along with the jewels, of course—many people come in search of spirits. Curious visitors as well as serious researchers hope to come face-to-face (or face to space, in the case of the tower's many headless apparitions) with a genuine ghost.

These aren't your run-of-the-mill apparitions, either. Many bluebloods linger there, long after their mortal existence. Although the tower served as a grim prison for most of its history, it didn't house common criminals. Being locked up in its gray stone walls was a privilege reserved mainly for those who posed a direct threat to the Crown.

And so we find the likes of old Henry VI, imprisoned in the tower by Edward IV and knifed in 1471 while at prayer. Henry continues to pray, it is said, in a small chapel in Wakefield Tower. Anne Boleyn, second wife of Henry VIII, died in 1536 under the blade of a headsman specially imported from France for the occasion. Her crime: failing to provide the king with a male heir. Witnesses have reported seeing her walk the corridors carrying her own head in her hands. Every May 27, they say, the Countess of Salisbury reenacts her own execution (also ordered by Henry VIII). Apparently, she told the axman, "Come get me," before leading him on a chase around the fortress. Gallant swashbuckler and scholar Sir Walter Raleigh, too, still strolls along the battlement known as Raleigh's Walk.

Other ghosts in the tower can't be so easily identified. During the Second World War, for example, a sentry spotted two men in medieval uniforms walking back from Tower Hill, where the condemned often had their grisly sentences carried out. They bore an anonymous body, with its head tucked neatly beside it. In the 1960s, another sentry saw a cloaked figure appear out of nowhere and then vanish just as suddenly. He had trouble identifying this particular spirit on account of its headlessness.

Unlike these nobles and the nobodies, some tower ghosts don't take corporeal form at all. Take the Phantom

A ghost bear is said to stalk one of the halls in the notoriously haunted Tower of London.

Vial, which appeared before the family of Edmund Lenthal Swifte, keeper of the Crown Jewels, in October 1817.

The Swiftes were enjoying a pleasant dinner in their apartment in Martin Tower when Mrs. Swifte suddenly cried out in alarm and pointed at a spot in midair. Turning to look, Swifte saw an eerie glowing cylinder, approximately three inches in diameter, filled with what seemed to be swirling pale blue and white liquids. It drifted around the room and eventually passed behind Mrs. Swifte. "Oh Christ!" she screamed, "it has seized me!" Swifte threw a wooden chair at the mysterious canister and it disappeared. It hasn't been reported since.

This brings us to the Tower of London's resident ghost bear, which also stalks Martin Tower.

On a January night in 1815, with a chilling fog rolling off of the Thames, a young sentry patrolled the damp corridors of Martin Tower, keeping watch over the Crown Jewels. At the stroke of midnight, he saw, from out of the corner of his eye, a massive dark shape looming out of the Jewel Room's solid wooden door. He whirled around to find himself staring into the gaping jaws of a huge bear, snarling and bellowing in the ancient hallway.

More out of reflex than conscious thought, the sentry charged forward. He thrust his bayonet, but it passed straight through the fearsome apparition. Instead, he ended up driving the blade more than an inch into the sturdy oak of the door. He tugged at his weapon frantically, but couldn't withdraw it. Disarmed and terrified, he did the natural thing: he fainted.

It wasn't until the following afternoon that he revived somewhat, barely coherent and clearly suffering from severe mental shock. He managed to tell his incredible story, in a halting voice that was more babble than speech. Edmund Lental Swifte, who would battle the floating cylinder a year later, recorded the tale. That night the addled young sentry lapsed back into semi-consciousness. The next day he passed away, dead from fright.

It might seem odd to find a bear in the tower, keeping company with the unhappy spirits of fallen nobles and inconvenient cousins. But the tower's long, strange history holds a clue to its origins.

In 1235, King Henry III received a gift of three African leopards. For the next 600 years, the aptly named Lion Tower housed the Royal Menagerie.

While it operated, the Royal Menagerie provided such spectacles as the first African elephant in Britain since the Roman occupation a millennium earlier. In the 18th century, blood-thirsty visitors flocked to the spectacle of the big cats' feeding time. In lieu of paying cash admission, visitors could bring a dog or cat to be fed to the lions and leopards.

But where does our snarling phantom bear fit in? It may be the image of a Norwegian polar bear once housed at the menagerie. It used to take daily swims in the Thames, at the end of a long tether. More likely, the spirit is a holdover from the brutal Bear Pits, first established by James I.

Bear baiting, a cruel and gruesome diversion, was very popular at the time. Bears, driven mad by taunting and poor treatment, were chained to a pole in a pit to be attacked by dogs or even tigers while spectators cheered. The bears rarely came out on the winning side.

Animals can feel fear and pain as deeply as humans do, and these emotions figure largely in many hauntings. Like the human victims in the Tower of London, these bears suffered harsh imprisonment and cruel execution. Perhaps it's only fitting that one of them should stalk the cold stone halls and bellow its undying rage.

The Ghost Dog
of Ballechin Manor

It was a dreary, windy afternoon in Strathay, Scotland, nearly 130 years ago. John Stuart stood in the study of Ballechin House, a property he'd inherited upon the recent death of his uncle, and took a long drink of whiskey to steady his nerves. Not a drinker by habit, he nonetheless felt the need for "liquid courage" for the task at hand: to pick up his hunting rifle, go out to the kennels and shoot all 14 of his uncle's beloved hounds.

What could drive an otherwise sane and righteous man to such a horrific act? For the answer, we must look to John Stuart's uncle himself.

Robert Stuart (sometimes spelled Steuart) was born in the newly built Ballechin House in 1806. At the age of 19, he followed in the footsteps of many young men of his time and sought his fortune with the East India Company. After 25 years, he finally returned to Ballechin and retired holding the rank of major. He had a heavy limp, thanks to an old bullet wound to the knee.

Since the house had been leased to tenants, Major Stuart was obliged to live for some time in a smaller cottage elsewhere on the property. He soon developed a local reputation as an eccentric, to say the least. Despising the company of other humans, he much preferred his large pack of dogs.

Few people ever saw him, with the exception of his young housekeeper, Sarah. When she died mysteriously in 1873 at the age of 27, the stories really began to fly. Rumor had it that her body was found in the major's bed, rather than her quarters, as would have been appropriate.

We'll never know for certain what went on in Ballechin House, although the stories of violence, sadism and weird occult rituals don't paint a cheerful picture.

No doubt many of the locals' speculations were based on the major's strange spiritual beliefs. A deeply religious man, Major Stuart absorbed many elements of Eastern mysticism into his personal philosophy during his quarter-century in India. Chief among these was a firm belief in transmigration—the soul's ability to move to another body after death. He vowed that his soul would return to Ballechin to live again in the body of his favorite dog, a magnificent black spaniel.

This promise—or threat—of a return from beyond the grave led John Stuart, a devout Roman Catholic, to perform his bloody deed on that afternoon in 1874. Offended, embarrassed and terrified by his uncle's unorthodox beliefs, the younger Stuart didn't take any chances. He slaughtered the dogs, had the major's old cottage blessed by the local priest and turned it over to the church as a prayer retreat for nuns.

Not long afterwards, mysterious events began to occur at Ballechin House. Stuart's wife was the first to experience the phenomena. Alone one morning in the major's former study, still working to get her husband and herself comfortably settled in the new place, she suddenly noticed a strong animal scent in the room, like the smell of a damp hunting dog. As she opened the windows in a vain attempt to air out the foul-smelling study, she felt an unseen dog brush past her.

This was the first of a long string of weird events, most of which will sound familiar to anyone who's read about haunted places—strange knocks and raps (some so loud they were interpreted as gunshots), inexplicable cold spots and indistinct phantom voices that seemed to be arguing angrily. Through it all were reports of a sudden strong scent of dog and the feeling of a hound's muzzle or flank at witnesses' legs.

A frequent visitor to Ballechin House, a Jesuit priest by the name of Father Hayden, encountered the house's ghost dog several times. The priest often woke in the middle of the night to the sound of a dog scratching at the door to his guest room, as if wanting to be let in. Each time Father Hayden opened the door, the hall was empty and silent and smelled faintly of damp fur.

In 1895, John Stuart was crushed under the wheels of a London cab. Some say his death was heralded by three sharp raps on the walls of his study and the barking of dogs outside.

A family by the name of Heaven next rented Ballechin House, entering into a one-year lease. Unfortunately for them, the forces at work in the old house picked that time to increase the intensity of their activities.

Ballechin's resident phantom canine decided to make himself seen as well as heard, felt and smelled. Family members described fleeting glimpses of a mysterious black shadow and a dark dog-like shape. The apparition was joined by a new otherworldly visitor, a mournful-looking woman in a white dress, whose appearances were accompanied by the sound of rustling silk. Was this the spirit of Sarah, the housekeeper who died in the major's bed?

The major himself also apparently rejoined his former lover and faithful hound. Late one night, one of Mr. Heaven's daughters woke to the drag-stomp sound of heavy, limping footsteps circling her bed—the very bed where the major slept and Sarah died. Already frightened by prior events in the house, the poor girl screamed in terror. Family members who rushed into her room also heard the crippled footsteps.

The spirits of Ballechin House began to assert themselves more forcefully and physically. Doors banged open and closed on their own, bedsheets and curtains were torn off or twisted, the arguing phantom voices became louder and more threatening and the sound of barking and growling grew more frequent. Finally, after barely three months of tenancy, the Heavens forfeited the nine months' rent they'd already paid and vacated the house.

By this time, Ballechin House had built up quite a reputation as a haunted house. It attracted the attention of the Marquis of Bute, vice-president of Britain's Society for Psychical Research (SPR). He made arrangements to rent Ballechin at his own expense and sent an SPR member named Colonel Taylor there to conduct an investigation. In addition to Taylor and his family, scores of SPR members and other guests stayed at Ballechin during this time.

The "investigation" was neither rigorous nor methodical. At times, the house was packed with over 40 assorted spiritualists and curiosity seekers who seemed more intent on a lovely Scottish vacation on Lord Bute's tab than on revealing the secrets of the haunting. Nevertheless, many guests reported mysterious knocks, shouts, gunshots, barks and other noises during their nights at Ballechin. They reported various visual apparitions as well.

One medium in particular, Miss Ada Goodrich, claimed to have had spiritual contact with one of the ghosts of Ballechin. She described a nun named Ishbel whose face, she said, appeared to be "in mental pain, so that perhaps it is hardly fair to say that it seems lacking in that repose and gentleness that one looks for in the religious life." Could this "Ishbel" have in fact been John Stuart's late sister, Isabella? Isabella had entered the religious life and, as Sister Frances Helen, had frequently visited the prayer retreat her brother had established.

The sloppy, chaotic nature of the SPR's investigation opened the door to criticism and debunking. The case was debated and ridiculed in the pages of the *Times*. SPR houseguest J. Callender Ross wrote, "The only mystery in the matter seems to be the mode in which an ordinary dwelling was endowed with so evil a reputation." Even formerly terrified tenant Mr. Heaven claimed that he had believed all along that Ballechin's mysterious noises were caused by "hot water pipes." He blamed his overly superstitious womenfolk for inducing him to abandon his lease, writing off nearly a year's worth of rent.

Whatever "reality" was claimed for Ballechin House, its "evil reputation" prevented it from being occupied for any length of time. By 1932 the old house, decrepit and unloved, had become unfit for human habitation. Beyond restoration, it stood empty, slowly sliding back into the earth, until it was finally demolished in 1963.

Gef, the Talking Mongoose

The Isle of Man, just northwest of England, isn't known for its cosmopolitan bustle. Sparsely populated and mostly rural, the 220-square-mile island sees little excitement apart from the summer months, when boatloads of travelers and tourists arrive to enjoy the windswept moors and picturesque rocky coastlines.

For a brief period in the early 1930s, though, the eyes of the world turned toward a tiny stone farmhouse in the south of the island. Journalists, researchers, psychologists and spiritualists converged on the Irving family's home in search of one of the strangest creatures ever seen: a mischievous talking mongoose who called himself Gef.

For seven long years, the Irvings shared their home with this amazing (and often obnoxious) beast. Gef swore like a sailor, spied on the neighbors, threw small objects, pilfered food and, when he was upset, urinated on guests through cracks in the walls and ceiling.

Every investigator who visited the Irving home came away with a different theory on Gef's origins. Some thought him a ghost or spirit. Others suggested he might be a genuine elf or fairy. Some suggested he was a poltergeist. Others were satisfied to accept Gef as what he claimed to be—an 80-year-old mongoose who had learned to talk. Of course, many more were convinced "Gef" was a hoax. Whatever they thought, nearly all investigators agreed upon the creature's close connection to the Irvings' 12-year-old daughter, Viorrey.

Life on the isolated moors could be lonely for an only child. With few neighbors and fewer playmates, Viorrey spent her days running wild in the hills. She hunted rabbits with her dog, Mona, and imagined herself in the fantastic faraway places she'd heard about from her widely traveled father, James. She also dreamt up imaginary friends. At first this was all Gef seemed to be.

But not long after Viorrey first mentioned Gef to her mother and father, matter-of-factly crediting the little predator for her rabbit kills, strange things began to occur in the Irving home.

The stone house had interior wood paneling, with a gap between the inner and outer walls. Strange noises began to emanate from the walls—thumps, scratches, knocks, growls, chattering and catlike wails. The noises centered around Viorrey's room and in the ceiling above the stairway leading to the second floor.

Within a few months, James noticed that some of the noises were beginning to sound like human speech. Then, on a day when Gef was being particularly rambunctious, James exclaimed to his wife, "What in the name of God can he be?" A second later he heard his words repeated from inside the walls, in a rodent-like chattering voice pitched far higher than a woman's or even a girl's. Gef had spoken for the first time, and the Irvings' lives would never be the same.

Once Gef picked up the habit of talking, he never let it drop. He mimicked voices, teased and swore, often using choice French and Italian phrases James had picked up. Gef also threw things at people (with uncanny aim), knocked objects off of high shelves and generally made a nuisance of himself. His mischief became so frequent and intense that James, fearing for his daughter's safety, resolved to exterminate the pest. When Gef learned of this plan, he unleashed a ferocious barrage of howls, screams and curses. The frightened Irvings moved Viorrey into their bedroom for her protection.

Eventually, the Irvings reached a truce with their invisible lodger. Mrs. Irving began to set out small morsels of food for Gef, and he repaid the favor by killing rabbits and leaving them on the doorstep. The impoverished Irvings certainly welcomed this bit of "rent."

Gef became like a strange family member, temperamental but protective. He played occasional pranks, told stories about his adventures around the island and gossiped about the neighbors. Yet he always remained invisible to everyone but Viorrey. On the one occasion when she caught a good look at Gef, she described him as bushy-tailed, with yellowish-brown fur, a flat face and forepaws that seemed more like little hands than animal feet—not at all like a mongoose.

When asked why he never showed himself to the rest of the family, or to visitors, Gef would reply, "You'd catch me and put me in a bottle."

As Gef's notoriety spread, investigators, journalists and curiosity seekers began to make their way to the Irvings' little farmstead. Gef rarely disappointed his audiences. He performed little tricks, such as calling a coin heads or tails by peering down through cracks in the ceiling, and became more and more talkative.

James Irving was in his glory. An educated and well-traveled man, Irving sometimes felt trapped by his poverty and isolation. The company of so many cultured conversationalists was a balm to Irving's starved soul. His obvious social neediness, however, made it easy for some investigators to declare the phenomenon a hoax. Gef, they said, was nothing more than a figment of a lonely girl's imagination, exploited by a father who craved attention.

In the face of such skepticism, Gef became increasingly moody. He felt insulted by doubters and frequently refused to speak in their presence.

Some researchers believed in Gef's existence, but saw him as a paranormal manifestation of the household's psychological intensity. In her book *Haunted People*, psychiatrist Nandor Fodor hypothesized that Gef grew out of James Irving's need to feed his mental starvation, combined with Viorrey's need to please and support her father.

Whatever Gef was or wasn't, by 1938 his brief fame was over. Irving, in a desperate bid to keep the publicity alive, provided samples of Gef's fur—but these were found to exactly match that of Viorrey's dog, Mona. "Ventriloquism hoax" became the standard theory behind the strange events in the little stone house on the moors. The Irvings sold their farmstead—at a disappointing price owing to its haunted reputation—and moved elsewhere.

The Star Inn's Ghost Dog

Many people believe that dogs and other animals surpass humans in their ability to detect ghosts and other spectral phenomena. In haunted places, dogs often bark or growl at nothing, or otherwise behave strangely. This in itself doesn't prove much; dogs bark at nothing all the time.

At the Star Inn at Ingatestone, Essex, however, visiting Fidos and Rovers seem to bark at the spirit of a long-dead guard dog.

The Star Inn is the kind of place you imagine when you hear the words "English pub"—cozy and picturesque, warm and woody, with a roaring fire in the hearth year-round and good ale served from the cask. As you look up from your pint, however, you'll see something you won't find in any other pub. The stuffed head of a fierce bull terrier hangs above the bar, keeping watch over the house.

From 1900 to 1914, the terrier served as the inn's guard dog. A legendary scrapper, he never lost a fight. When at last the old warrior died of old age, the owner honored his memory by making the dog's head a permanent part of the bar's decor. This proved to be more than a symbolic gesture, since the terrier's spirit appears to have remained to guard the pub through the years.

This ghost dog seems to reserve his energy for scaring off other dogs. Many dog owners have tried to lead their faithful pups through the passage leading to the bar, only to have them back away, snarling and staring at empty air. They behave precisely as if they had been challenged by another, more aggressive dog.

A former landlord described his own dog's reaction: "She growled, stiffened and up went her bristles like a hedgehog. She was not only threatening something, but was being threatened herself. She was dead scared."

While alive, the Star Inn's guard dog had no love of other canines, to put it mildly. Today, such a savage fighter would be put down as a menace. He showed no love for thieves and other intruders, either. And while no human has reported seeing the ghost, it seems the old dog may still be scaring away criminals on some subconscious level. Although pubs are a prime target for Essex's break-and-enter artists, the Star Inn has never been burgled.

A Weird Menagerie

Most animal phantoms, however elusive, tend to be fairly stable. An area said to be haunted by a mysterious black dog, say, won't suddenly produce reports of spectral white horses. But every rule has its exceptions, with ghosts as with all things. Take the English country village of Hoe Benham, for example. For a time in the early 20th century, one of its tree-shaded lanes hosted a whole menagerie of spirits.

In the summer of 1903, two London artists, Oswald Pittman and Reginald Waud, took up residence in a small cottage in Hoe Benham. They invited another friend, Clarissa Miles, to join them there for a weekend of painting in the sunny countryside. As Oswald and Reginald sat at their easels in the garden, they saw

Clarissa coming down the lane. They were surprised to see, following her, a huge white pig with an extraordinarily long snout.

When Clarissa reached the cottage, Reginald asked that she please leave her pig outside the gate, as he was worried the animal would damage his flowers and vegetables. At first, Clarissa thought this must be some kind of strange joke. She had certainly not brought a pig with her, and if one had been trailing her she would have heard its footsteps and snuffling. Her friends insisted that they were serious, and together they went down to the lane to investigate. They found no sign of the animal, only Clarissa's footprints in the dusty road.

Perplexed, they began asking nearby villagers about the strange pig, but none of them had seen it on the road that day. In fact, they said, if they had seen a pig wandering loose they would have put it down immediately, since there was swine fever in that district. But although none had spotted the large white pig, many reported seeing different inexplicable apparitions at other times. As the three artists continued along the lane, they uncovered all kinds of strange stories.

Several farmers recounted seeing a large white animal approximately the size of the pig that had followed Clarissa. Some called it "sheeplike" while others said it was "somewhat like a calf." The animal was sometimes accompanied by a buzzing noise or high-pitched whine, and always vanished before the farmers' startled eyes. One man described striking the creature with his walking stick, causing it to blink out of existence—or at least out of sight.

Another man, a farm laborer, described returning from the fields with his eight-man crew. As the wagons passed along the lane, the horses suddenly became nervous. Above the animals' heads appeared a strange white orb, bobbing and dancing in midair. After hovering over the cart for some distance, the orb suddenly floated up over the gate of a roadside fence and disappeared.

Another farmer had an eerie nighttime encounter at that same spot in the road. On his way home on a clear, moonlit night, he was startled by a large black animal crouching near the gate. He cautiously approached the animal, thinking it was a farm dog that had wandered away from its home. As he drew near, the doglike creature suddenly doubled or tripled in size and transformed into a "black donkey." It unleashed a bloodcurdling shriek— part hound's howl, part hog's squeal and part horse's whinny—reared up and bounded away over the fence, leaving the petrified farmer shivering in the lane.

The locals had their own theory regarding these apparitions. In the mid-1700s, a man by the name of King committed suicide on the farm bordering the lane. Though his farmhouse and other buildings had long since tumbled down, and their stones had been reused in the fences of other area farmers, the area was still known as King Farm. Oswald and Reginald's neighbors believed that the dark force haunting the stretch of lane was the result of King's suicide—or, perhaps, the cause of it.

Intrigued by these stories, the three friends decided to conduct their own firsthand investigation. Like many in London's artistic set at the turn of the century, they considered themselves amateur spiritualists. One evening they "opened their senses to the spirit world" and walked down the haunted lane. As they passed the spot where the King farmstead had stood, Clarissa immediately felt overwhelmed by an evil force.

Absolutely certain that this malicious entity intended to do them harm, Clarissa shouted at her friends to flee the area. As they scrambled frantically back towards their cottage, they heard an unearthly scream—part hound's howl, part hog's squeal, part horse's whinny…and part human wail.

A Saint's Faithful Friend

Holy men and women share a strange connection with other living creatures. Cultures in every corner of the earth have tales of monks, hermits and saints with mystical links to the world of animals. One of the most spectacular of these took place in relatively modern times— Grigio, the phantom protector of Saint Giovanni Bosco.

Born in Becchi, Italy, in 1815, Don Bosco ("Don" is a title of respect applied to priests and noblemen) spent his life working with poor, orphaned and delinquent boys in the slums of Turin. He had a gift for saving children whom society had relegated to the gutters, bringing many of them to the priesthood.

Don Bosco was also physically powerful, a gifted athlete and an amateur acrobat. His strength served him well in Valdocco, the crime-ridden quarter where he did much of his work.

But even the strongest man would be a fool to wander the dark, stinking alleys of Valdocco alone, especially a man in Don Bosco's position. Along with the usual hoodlums and muggers, he had to guard against the anger and resentment of established church and civic authorities. He knew they weren't above using strong-arm tactics—even murder—to put an end to his "rabble-rousing" social work.

Still, on a dark night in 1852, the future saint decided to risk a long, solitary walk home through the maze of seedy taverns, squatters' shacks and open sewers. Striding quickly along the dank streets, Don Bosco prayed for safe passage, regretting his decision to travel alone.

Suddenly, a huge, furry form leaped from the shadows. A German shepherd, three feet high at the shoulders, stood on the path, its shining gray coat standing out against the dingy slum street. Ordinarily, a strange dog in Valdocco posed a greater threat than any armed robber—the district was plagued by starving feral strays. For some reason, though, the lone priest felt no fear.

Don Bosco later recalled the incident in his memoirs, *A Mysterious Dog: Grigio*. The dog's manner, he wrote, "was not threatening. It was rather like a dog that had recognized its master. We quickly became friends." The strange canine accompanied him safely home before vanishing back into the darkness.

After that, the priest frequently found himself escorted and protected by the dog, whom he named Grigio, which means "gray" in Italian.

If Grigio had been an illusion, Don Bosco would have denounced him as such. Although deeply spiritual, open to God's many unknowable mysteries, he had no time for ghost stories, bugaboos and bogeymen. Yet one of the best-loved stories of the saint's early life has him doing a bit of paranormal investigation and ghostbusting.

One of these involves the precocious Giovanni, not yet 10 years old, visiting the home of his maternal grandparents in the village of Capriglio. Everyone was having a fine time when one of Giovanni's cousins bolted down from the upstairs bedrooms, obviously frightened.

"Something's making noises in the attic," he stammered, his face white. "There's a ghost in the house!"

Two of Giovanni's uncles went upstairs to investigate and came back to confirm that they too heard weird noises. Perhaps owing to the young cousin's premature mention of the word "ghost," the family's collective imagination began to spin out of control.

"It sounds like the shuffling and stamping of feet," said one of the uncles, "as if someone was hitting the floor with a stick." The noises, he said, seemed to follow him as he went from room to room. By this time, even the adults felt their spines tingling. No one knew what to do next.

No one, that is, except cocky little Giovanni. "Why not go up into the attic to see what's going on?" he suggested.

"Are you out of your mind?" his grandmother cried. "You're not going up there, and neither is anyone else! At least not tonight, not in the dark." The rest of the family shared her sentiment. Sure, it's probably nothing, but why take chances? Who knows what nastiness might lurk in the blackness?

Giovanni remained adamant. "Look, we have to do something!" he said. "We can't just sit down here and worry until morning. Who's coming with me?" With that, he grabbed a lamp off the table and began ascending the steep wooden stairway. The men in the room, stung that a nine-year-old boy displayed more courage than all of them put together, followed him in a gaggle up the stairs.

The first of the menfolk tentatively poked his head and shoulders through the attic hatch, peering around the cramped space in the uncertain light cast by Giovanni's lamp. He saw a large cornmeal sieve, erratically sliding and jerking across the rough wood floor as if pulled and batted by invisible hands.

"Get back, Giovanni, get back!" he cried. "It's a ghost! It's the devil!" The rest of the men clustered below him fell over each other in a mad rush back down the stairs.

Giovanni merely laughed and strode unafraid into the attic. He stooped, lifted the heavy sieve and revealed the "ghost"—a big old rooster, its feathers ruffled, blinking in the sudden light. With a big smile, the young boy picked up the bedraggled fowl. "Here's your ghost, Uncle," he laughed, holding up the rooster.

Relief and embarrassment washed over the entire family. Now that the terrifying "ghost" had been unmasked, they pieced together a rational explanation. The poor rooster, one of a large flock that roamed the property, had found its way into the attic. Pecking around for trapped morsels of corn, it had toppled the sieve onto itself. Everyone heartily congratulated Giovanni on his clear-headedness.

Now, as an adult, Don Bosco remained equally clear-headed. But Grigio was no ordinary dog, nor was he a figment of a frightened imagination. Over the next four decades, hundreds of students, citizens and clergy saw and touched the mysterious dog. His origins may have been unknown, his appearances and disappearances uncanny, but those who encountered the fearsome Grigio—especially those with harm in their hearts—had no doubt that they were dealing with a real dog.

One miserably cold and wet November night, two years after Grigio's first appearance, Don Bosco once again headed home without a companion. He carefully chose a heavily traveled route but, as it turns out, his fellow pedestrians were not quite as righteous as he.

"At one point I noticed two men walking a short distance in front of me, matching their pace with mine," Don Bosco wrote. "I crossed over to the other side to avoid them but they did the same. I then tried to turn back but it was too late. They wheeled around and were upon me in two steps. Without a word they threw some kind of coat over me. I struggled in vain to break loose. One of them then tried to gag me with a scarf. I wanted to shout, but I hadn't the strength."

From out of nowhere Grigio appeared, hurling his massive fanged bulk at the two thugs and "growling like a bear." He held his massive paws on the throat of one man, while snarling at the other. The robbers quickly lost all interest in the contents of their victim's coin purse. They begged the priest to call off his dog.

"I'm going to," Don Bosco replied, "but next time, leave strangers alone!"

Grigio stood snarling by the priest's side, his teeth bared and hackles raised, until the would-be muggers fled from sight. Don Bosco made it home safely that night, and from then on, "every evening when I went out alone I always noticed Grigio by the side of the road."

Like all good bodyguards, Grigio could sense a threat even before it emerged. Late one evening, Don Bosco remembered some urgent business he had left unattended in the city center. His mother urged him not to travel at such a late hour, but he insisted he had to go. After calling for volunteers to accompany him, he headed out. At the gate, however, he found Grigio stretched across the threshold, barring his path.

"He's been there quite a while," one of his staff told him. "We tried to get rid of him a couple of times, even took a stick to him, but he kept coming back." The crusading priest just laughed. "You don't have to worry about Grigio," he said. "Now I can leave without fear!" He reached down to give the dog a friendly pat and scratch behind the ears. "Come on, Grigio," he said. "Let's get going!"

Grigio snarled in reply, causing Don Bosco to snatch his hand back. "Don't you know me anymore, Grigio?" he asked, shocked. He tried to step over or around the dog, and got the same response. The boys with Don Bosco tried shouting and tossing pebbles, but the huge shaggy dog refused to budge.

Don Bosco's mother, came out to see what all the fuss was about. Seeing Grigio's determined stand, she scolded her son. "If you won't listen to your mother," she said, "at least listen to the dog. He has more sense than you!"

Reluctantly, Don Bosco abandoned his plans to travel. Grigio rose from the doorstep, stretched and trotted off into the night. Less than 20 minutes later, a friend ran breathlessly into the yard with an urgent warning.

"Don't let Don Bosco go out tonight!" he shouted. "Three or four men are hiding out in the house at the end of the street in ambush. They've sworn to kill Don Bosco as soon as he leaves the school!"

Years later, Don Bosco finally outlasted his opposition and established his mission. Although the priest no longer faced the nightly threat of robbery or intimidation, Grigio still appeared occasionally to guide and protect him when he was lost and alone.

Over the years, Don Bosco's associates tried unsuccessfully to determine where Grigio came from, and where he went. But the old priest never shared their curiosity. In his memoirs, he wrote, "What does it matter? What matters is, he was my friend."

The Boy Who Drew Cats

Retold from a Japanese legend collected in Gleanings from Buddha-Fields, *by Lafcadio Hearn, 1897*

Oishi-san put his hands on his hips and looked around the dishevelled storeroom in exasperation. Jars, rice bales and other containers had been stacked and arranged, but sloppily. Some teetered on the edge, while others stood with their lids cocked half open. The floor had been hastily swept. Despite the relatively clean patch in the center of the room, the corners remained littered with dust, straw and stray grains of rice. The poor farmer sighed. This was the kind of half-hearted work he'd come to expect from his youngest son.

And where was little Yukio, now that he'd "finished" his assigned chores? The farmer knew the answer all too well. The boy was no doubt off somewhere, playing with his beloved cats.

That boy and his cats! Oishi-san thought angrily as he picked up the broom and set about finishing his son's chores. If Yukio had his own way, he would spend every waking hour with his four-footed friends. And when he wasn't playing with cats he'd be daydreaming by the canal or playing strange make-believe games by himself. Anything but farm work! Sometimes the farmer imagined that his son was a half-cat, a changeling given to him by mischievous animal spirits as a cruel prank.

The farmer's other children weren't at all like Yukio. His eldest son, at only 14 years old, was already almost a man, a strong, dependable farmboy who did his work diligently and without complaining. The two middle sisters were likewise well-behaved. They helped their mother well in household tasks and showed every sign of growing into perfectly respectable young women.

But Yukio…ah! He wasn't a bad child, or stupid; on the contrary, he was far brighter than his brothers and sisters. But he could not keep his energetic mind focused on the dreary physical labor of farm life. Even when he did get down to work, he wasn't much good at it. A small, frail boy, Yukio tired quickly and was prone to injury. What to do with a boy like this?

Oishi-san and his wife agreed that his son had no happy future in farming. "I could punish him, beat him, force him to conform to this work," the farmer said. "That would be my right, and maybe my duty, as his father. But what good would that do? In all other ways, Yukio is a joy to me. I can't force him into a life to which he's so clearly unsuited. It would be like a carpenter forcing a poorly matched joint together by hammering it. The finished piece isn't worth the work!"

"You're right, husband," his wife replied. "And besides, he's so clever. He needs more to think about than sowing and reaping rice. Without something to occupy his mind, who knows what kind of mischief he'll eventually get up to?

"Perhaps he'd make a good apprentice at the temple," she continued. "The priest is getting old. Maybe he'll take our clever son on as an acolyte." The farmer thought this suggestion was excellent, and the next day the couple brought little Yukio to the temple to meet the priest.

It was cold and drizzling the morning they approached the temple. Yukio, much to his father's annoyance, clung close to his mother's side as they walked up the rain-slicked granite steps. He didn't really understand what was going on. He only knew that the priest wanted to speak with him and that—as his mother had blurted out—if he was very polite and answered all the priest's questions correctly, he'd never have to do farm work again. So, with a mixture of anxiety and boyish hope he entered the strange building, its air heavy with incense.

After greeting the parents, the old priest drew Yukio away to speak with the young boy privately. He asked him a series of difficult and intricate questions in order to test his wit and intelligence. Though he hadn't expected much from one so young—simply speaking politely and not crying out for his mother would probably have sufficed—the priest was amazed by Yukio's creativity and insight and his polite, well-spoken manner. Pleased to have been blessed with such a promising young student, the priest brought Yukio back out and announced to the happy parents that he would accept the boy into the temple.

"I have just one condition, young man," said the priest, drawing himself up and doing his best to fill his voice with authoritarian thunder. He had heard that the boy was difficult, and he was determined to make an early impression.

"Here in this temple," the priest continued, "I am the master. If you are to remain here, you must swear to obey me in all things, or be turned out. Do you swear to obey me?"

Yukio bowed very deeply and tried to keep his voice from shaking as he replied. "Yes, teacher. I swear!"

The boy's father puffed with pride and his mother tried to hold back tears as the old priest turned and led Yukio into the temple precincts. "Excellent," he said. "Now hurry up and follow me. You have much to learn, and the day is almost half over!"

The boy tried diligently to honor his vow of obedience. He worked harder in the temple than he ever had on his parents' farm. He soaked up his lessons like a sponge, impressing the old priest and the other acolytes with his quick-witted intelligence. Visitors to the temple were shocked when this small boy, seemingly little more than an infant, greeted them in such polite and mature tones. Everyone believed Yukio would go far.

There was just one problem. At the temple, Yukio had free access to brushes and ink for the first time in his young life. Writing materials were far too expensive for a poor farm family to afford. Here, though, writing and drawing lay at the heart of everyday life. Paper was plentiful and ink ran like a river, and Yukio soon discovered a talent and fondness for drawing. Perhaps "obsession" would be a better word, for the little farm boy focused his art on one subject exclusively: the cats and kittens he loved so much.

Whenever Yukio had time to himself, time he should have spent studying his lessons or practicing the intricate art of Japanese writing, he drew cats. Old cats and frisky kittens, cats with long tails and cats with no tails, black cats and white cats, cats fighting and cats sleeping, cats hunting and cats eating—hundreds of cats, on every available scrap of paper.

These weren't childish doodles, either. Yukio had an incredible natural talent, and his love of felines had made him a very keen observer of their behavior and movement. Each of his countless cat drawings was a minor masterpiece. The cats seemed to leap off the page. Everyone who saw them was amazed that an untrained child could dash off such vivid and subtle work.

But, masterpieces or not, drawings of cats should not occupy the time of a young temple apprentice. As bright as he was, Yukio had fallen behind in his studies, and the marvel of his illustrations had begun to disturb the serenity of the temple. Finally, the old priest called the boy into his chamber to address the issue.

"You swore to obey me in all things, Yukio," he declared, "and yet you don't study. Instead, you spend all your time drawing pictures. I hereby order you to stop this disruption. From now on, you will study when it is time to study and not waste time doodling. Do you understand?"

"Yes, teacher," replied the cowering boy. "I will obey."

"Hmm. See that you do. Otherwise, I shall have no choice but to turn you out of the temple."

As an extra precaution, the priest decreed that Yukio would no longer have free access to paper. From now on he would have to request and justify each sheet. That should settle matters, thought the old priest, anxious to see his promising young student live up to his potential.

But Yukio had an artist's soul. He tried to master his passion, but it overwhelmed him. Cats just kept coming to his mind, demanding to be brought to life. He continued to draw on every scrap of paper he could lay his hands on. When there was no paper to be had, he drew cats on the undersides of tables, on pieces of wood and fragments of cloth—on any flat surface that would stay still for his brush. Finally, though, the compulsive young artist dared to draw on the inviting pure white surface of the temple's rice-paper screens. This was the last straw.

Once again, Yukio found himself called in front of the priest. The old man was saddened by what he had to do. The boy was the most intelligent student the temple had ever seen, and there was no doubt that he was a gifted artist. But rules were rules. The temple had no place for a frenzied scribbler who lacked the obedience and propriety to keep from covering every available surface with cat drawings. *No matter how beautiful they are,* the priest sighed to himself.

"Young man," the priest intoned, "the first rule of a temple acolyte is obedience. Twice you swore to obey me in all things, and twice you have disobeyed. I had hoped for better from you, but you have left me with no choice. I hereby expel you from the temple. Pack up your belongings and return to your family."

Struck by a strange and sudden inspiration, the old priest added, "As you leave here forever, I offer you one final piece of guidance. I say to you, avoid large places at night; keep to the small. Buddha bless you, Yukio." With that, the priest turned and entered his private chamber, sliding the screen closed with solid finality.

Yukio stood there, almost in tears. Where would he go? His family would be angry and ashamed if he returned to the farm, and he'd surely be punished for disobeying the old priest and wasting the chance he'd been given.

Instead, the little boy bravely decided to head for the big city nearby. He knew of a grand temple there, with many priests. Certainly they would have a place for one more willing young apprentice. Shouldering his bag, he set off down the road.

At first, he enjoyed the journey immensely. It was a beautiful day, and the trees, birds and insects delighted his curious eyes and mind. He walked along, filled with childish hopes and dreams of the adventure that lay before him. He even met a couple of cats along the way and spent time playing with each. Because of his leisurely pace, he didn't arrive at the gates of the city until late at night.

By this time, Yukio was tired, hungry and more than a little afraid. Although the city was only 12 miles from his home, it was farther than he'd ever been in his life. The streets were empty owing to the late hour, but he could see a welcoming golden light burning in the window of the big temple up on the hill. He hurried towards the light, hoping for sanctuary.

If he had arrived in the daytime, when there were people around, Yukio would have known that no sanctuary awaited him in the temple. It had recently fallen under an evil spell. A giant goblin rat had taken the place over, chasing out its frightened priests and raiding its storerooms. Soldiers and samurai had tried to rid the temple of the evil spirit, but physical weapons seemed to have no effect on the creature. Eventually the townsfolk gave up and abandoned their temple to the goblin. Since then, the crafty rat had kept the light burning at night to lure unsuspecting travelers such as Yukio.

The exhausted young artist trudged up the steps to the temple, dreaming of hot tea, white rice and maybe a little pickled plum. He knocked on the big wooden doors but received no answer. He knocked again, louder. Still no response. He pulled on the doors and they swung open, so Yukio decided to go in.

"Hello!" he called into the big, echoing interior of the temple. "Is anyone there?" He still heard no reply, but he expected that a priest would come by soon. He found a small chamber near the temple door and sat down to wait. He looked around the temple and noticed that it was very dusty and dirty. These priests could use an apprentice to clean up around here, Yukio thought, his spirits momentarily lightened.

But as his wait dragged on, still no priest or acolyte arrived. The boy began to feel restless and afraid. Gradually, the inevitable urge to draw came upon him. The white screens in this temple have very lovely surfaces, he thought. They're just begging for my brush. He found a writing box in a dusty corner of the room and set to work.

With the brush in his hands, his anxiety quickly melted away. As always, he comforted himself with his beloved cats. Feeling homesick, he began by drawing the cats he had played with at home. Then, feeling frightened, he depicted the farm's roughest, toughest cats. One was an old black cat with ragged ears, a grizzled veteran of hundreds of fights. Another was a champion mouser that kept the storeroom free of pests and fed countless litters of kittens in the process.

Yukio drew mother cats defending their young and kittens playfully learning to hunt. Surrendering to his compulsion, he kept drawing and drawing. Before long, he had completely covered the pristine screens of the deserted temple with a vibrant, living celebration of feline playfulness.

Finally, having painted more cats at once than he'd ever done, Yukio could barely hold the brush any longer. He lay down right on the floor of the temple and curled up to go to sleep. Just as he was about to close his eyes, though, he thought of the old priest's mysterious parting words: Avoid large places at night; keep to the small.

On the floor of the vast temple, Yukio felt suddenly vulnerable and exposed. He remembered seeing a cabinet in the small chamber he'd first visited. He went back and crawled into the cabinet, shutting the door behind him. It proved a perfect fit for his small frame, and he soon fell into a much-deserved sleep, resting his head on his little bundle of belongings.

Before long, though, he was awake. He heard a deafening commotion in the temple outside—screeching, growling and loud scuffling on the wooden floors. He heard paper being torn to shreds, huge statues being toppled and ceremonial vessels rolling across the floor. It sounded as if a pack of wild animals was fighting a monstrous battle right outside the cabinet door. Yukio huddled in the darkness.

Terrified but still curious, he carefully opened the cabinet door a crack and peered out into the temple. Somebody or something had extinguished the lamp, however, and Yukio could see nothing but thick blackness. Whimpering, the boy ducked back into his cabinet. He pulled his robe over his head, hoping to muffle the monstrous screeching and muffled banging outside, and prayed for his safety.

Somehow, despite the noise, the terrified child managed to fall asleep again. The next thing he knew, he awoke to an eerie silence. This time, when he opened the cabinet door he saw the morning light filtering through the dusty air. He cautiously climbed out of his cosy hiding place, tiptoed quietly across the reed mats that covered the chamber floor and went to peer into the temple's main hall. He saw something there that nearly made him jump back into his cabinet.

There, on the temple's dark wooden floor, Yukio saw the body of an enormous rodent. The evil goblin rat, bigger than two grown men, lay on the floor in a dark, glossy puddle, its body viciously sliced and punctured in dozens of places. What could have killed such a fearsome creature?

Then Yukio looked at the cats he had drawn on the walls. Each of them now had red flecks on its muzzle and whiskers. As he watched, the flecks were drying to a dark rust-brown.

The child now understood what had happened. His exquisite cats, each bearing the very soul and spirit of a precious farmyard friend, had saved him. They had somehow come to life to rescue the boy who loved them. Astounded and grateful, the polite and proper Yukio knelt and bowed low on the floor of the temple. He thanked the cat spirits and lord Buddha for delivering him from the foul creature that had haunted the place.

While Yukio prayed, the wary townspeople finally dared to open the doors of the temple they had abandoned. They had seen the temple's ever-present light go out in the night and had heard the wild screeching and yowling of the spirits' combat. They felt sure that another unfortunate stranger had been lured to his death in the temple. In order to give him proper last rites, they had come up the hill to gather the bones of the rat's latest victim. The town had enough troubles with a goblin rat without adding a restless ghost to the mix.

When they opened the door, though, they found a small boy kneeling beside the evil rat's corpse. The overjoyed villagers listened in amazement to the well-spoken young lad and his fantastic story.

The story soon spread throughout the district, and Yukio became a local hero. People from far and wide lined up to receive one of his cat drawings, famous both for their beauty and as charms against goblins and other evil spirits. The grateful priests of the now-reopened temple gladly took him in as an apprentice, letting him draw all the cats he wanted.

Little Yukio eventually became a famous artist, and both he and the temple prospered. Yukio grew old there, spending his days happily drawing, surrounded by his beloved cats.

2
Black Dogs

The Beast of Bungay

The town of Bungay, near Norwich, serves as the setting for one of the earliest and most shockingly violent published accounts of a Black Dog apparition. From Abraham Fleming's preface to his 1577 pamphlet, "A Strange and Terrible Wonder, Wrought Very Late in the Parish Church of Bongay," it's clear that he meant his account to serve as a dire reminder of the power of God's wrath.

"God warneth us by signs from heaven," Fleming writes, "by fiery appearances in the air most terrible; by wonders wrought on Earth, strange and unusual; by exinundations of waters beyond their appointed limits; by the removing of senseless trees from the natural place where they were planted; by the great power which the Prince of Darkness, through God's permission and sufferance, has recovered.

"God open the eyes of our hearts," he continues, after several lines prophesying calamity and destruction, "that we may see in what wildernesses, among what wild beasts and devouring serpents we do wander; and give us minds mollified and made soft, that all his works we may fear and be astonished."

Fleming chooses an effective context for his story: a dark and stormy night.

"Sunday, being the fourth of August, in the year of our Lord 1577, there fell from heaven an exceeding great and terrible tempest, sodden and violent, between nine o'clock in the morning and ten of the day aforesaid."

The rain fell in torrents, the huge, driving drops pelting the ground with "a wonderful force." The lanes ran with rivers of mud as the slashing tempest poured its countless gallons onto the town.

Along with the deluge came thunder and lightning, "the flashing of the one whereof was so rare and vehement, and the roaring noise of the other so forcible and violent, that it made not only people perplexed in mind and at their wits' end, but ministered such strange and unaccustomed cause of fear to be conceived, that dumb creatures…were exceedingly disquieted, and senseless things void of all life and feeling shook and trembled."

Under these terrible and ominous skies, in weather literally not fit for man or beast, the good people of Bungay and district gathered in the parish church for mass. The storm's violence, unprecedented in memory, provoked much worried discussion and debate. Many interpreted the tempest as a sure sign of God's displeasure and, dropping to their knees in worship, prayed with desperate intensity for deliverance.

Their prayers went unanswered. As mass commenced, the storm outside became even more intense. Thunder and lightning cracked and roared with such unearthly force that, to the assembled villagers, "the church did as it were quake and stagger, which struck into the hearts of those that were present such a sore and sudden fear that they in a manner were robbed of their right wits."

As the storm redoubled its fury outside, the atmosphere inside took on its own weird aspects. As Fleming writes, "Ye whole Church was so darkened, yea with such a palpable darkness, that one person could not perceive another, neither yet discern any light at all." The few candles and lamps gave off only the feeblest of glows, useless against the intangible black aura that filled the place of worship. The only light came from the stark electric flashes of the lightning that constantly split the sky outside.

At this point, with the gathered congregation praying in tearful fervor for God's mercy, there appeared, "in a most horrible similitude and likeness," a creature that seemed to spring straight out of Hell itself.

It was, writes Fleming, "a dog as they might discern it, of a black color…The sight thereof, together with the fearful flashes of fire which then were seen, moved such admiration in the minds of the assembly that they thought Doomsday was already come."

With glowing red eyes, surrounded by a flickering wreath of unearthly flame, the black dog ("or the devil in such a likeness") raced among the terrified churchgoers, with "great swiftness and incredible haste."

The dog passed between two people who had fallen to their knees in abject prayer. With two lightning-fast strikes from its powerful, slavering jaws, it "wrung the necks of them both at one instant clean backward, so that even at a moment where they kneeled, they strangely died."

At this shocking point in his narrative, the author takes the opportunity to repeat his main point. "This is a wonderful example of God's wrath," he explains, "no doubt to terrify us that we might fear him for his justice or, pulling back our footsteps from the paths of sin, to love him for his mercy."

But the black dog had not yet finished dispensing terrifying wonders to the people of Bungay. "Still continuing and remaining in one and the selfsame shape," the horrifying dark creature turned on another member of the congregation. Leaping on the luckless fellow's back, the dog savagely bit and tore at him with its talon-like claws before leaping off to continue its nightmare visitation.

Before the parishioners' unbelieving eyes, the man seemed to shrivel, wither and shrink, like "a piece of leather scorched in a hot fire; or as a mouth of a purse or bag, drawn together with string." Even more unbelievably, the stricken man did not die from his supernatural wounds. He survived, a withered and blasted human reminder of the horrible events, "which," Fleming writes, "is marvelous in the eyes of men, and offereth much matter of amazing the mind."

One other soul of Bungay encountered the black dog on that tempestuous day. In the midst of the fierce storm, the church caretaker had bravely (if unwisely) climbed up to the building's roof to clear the overflowing gutters, which threatened to flood or damage the church.

He struggled at his task, until "with a violent clap of thunder," he was hurled to the ground, lightning-struck. As he lay there, winded but unhurt, a huge black form loomed over him from out of the rain. Flaming red eyes glared at him for a terrifying moment, and the dog vanished into the impenetrable veil of pounding rain.

"At the time these things in this order happened," Fleming writes, "the rector or curate of the church, being partaker of the people's perplexity, comforted the people and exhorted them to prayer." The assembled congregation began again to pray earnestly; indeed, a good many of them had never stopped.

The hellish storm slackened to a more natural intensity, and the people of Bungay slowly collected their scattered wits. But the black dog continued its ominous itinerary. "On the self same day, in like manner" Fleming reports, "into the parish church of another town called Blibery [today's Blythburgh], not above seven miles distant…the like thing entered, in the same shape and similitude."

This time, the black dog appeared on an upper beam of the church, near the images of the Crucifix and the Holy Trinity. It stood before the startled congregation, snarling amid its unearthly halo of black fire.

"Suddenly it gave a swing down through the church, and there also, as before, slew two men and a lad, and burned the hand of another person who was there among the rest of the company, of whom [several] were blasted.

"This mischief thus wrought, it flew with wonderful force, to no little fear of the assembly, out of the church in a hideous and hellish likeness."

To corroborate his report ("which to some will seem absurd, although the sensibleness of the things itself confirmeth it to be truth"), Fleming describes the physical evidence at the scene, "as testimonies and the witnesses of the force which rested in this strange shaped thing." Several stones in the walls and floor of the church had cracked or shattered, he says, and the church door was torn. The church had suffered "ye marks as it were of its claws or talons." Furthermore, the machinery of the church's clock had been "wrung asunder and broken in pieces."

After stressing the gravity of his report—"These things are not lightly with silence to be over passed, but precisely and thoroughly to be considered"—Fleming once again urges his readers to regard the event as a divine warning and govern themselves accordingly.

"Let us pray unto God," he writes, "to work all things to the best, to turn our flinty hearts into fleshy hearts, that we may feel the fire of God's mercy, and flee from the scourge of his justice."

Did a terrifying supernatural Black Dog, divine or demonic, really appear to the people of Bungay? What really happened on that storm-wracked Sunday over 400 years ago?

The most likely explanation would be ball lightning. Severe storms sometimes produce floating globes of unearthly fire. Even today, scientists understand little about this atmospheric phenomenon. The frightened parishioners might easily have interpreted ball lightning as the embodiment of the devil dog from ancient folk legends. The burning, blasting and withering caused by the Black Dog, and even the broken necks—the result of the wild muscle spasms of electrocution—all fit the ball-lightning bill.

Of course, it's a little late to speculate on definitive answers. St. Mary's in Bungay no longer shows signs of the damage Fleming describes, although Holy Trinity in Blythburgh apparently still boasts a set of "devil's hoofprints."

In any case, the legend lives on. Bungay has adopted the Black Dog as the symbol of its civic identity, from the town crest (which prominently features a black hound) to the names of businesses and organizations, from the Black Dog Pub to the Black Dog Running Club. The good folk of Bungay, in other words, still pay tribute to that wild storm of long ago, when a terrifying something stalked their town.

The Legend of the Moddey Dhoo

St. Patrick's Isle, a tiny patch of rock off the Isle of Man, has an unexpectedly interesting history. Humans have occupied this rugged island for over 8000 years, since the hunter-gatherer tribes first came for its bountiful fishing and nearby fresh water. Over time, the isolated and easily defended island served as a secure storehouse, a place of refuge in times of trouble and a fortress for local kings. It is here that Saint Patrick himself—the missionary mystic traditionally credited with driving snakes out of Ireland—first brought Christianity to the Isle of Man, establishing a church and a monastery.

During the 10th century, 7000 years into the island's human history, marauding Vikings terrorized the region from their fearsome longships. Viking chieftain Magnus Barelegs established a stronghold and base on the isle to reprovision his raiding parties. In later centuries, the Scottish and English struggled bitterly over this strategic piece of isolated stone.

From the 14th to the 18th centuries, the English held solid claim on the island's fortress complex, by then known as Peel Castle. Late in this period, during the reign of Charles I, came the strangest chapter in the island's long history—when Peel Castle's cold stone corridors were stalked by the uncanny dark creature known as Moddey Dhoo (pronounced *mauther thoo*).

It was just after sunset, and the castle's gates had been locked for the night. The soldiers of the garrison took turns each evening carrying the key to the quarters of the captain of the guard, and tonight the chore fell to a certain young guardsman. Most of the soldiers looked forward to their turns. They enjoyed the air of ceremony, and also took advantage of the long walk to get in a bit of lollygagging.

Not so our sensible young guard. He feared and respected the unknown things that lurked in the twilight darkness. He had no great desire to wander the castle's damp passageways, far from the protective warmth of the guardroom's hearth. Worse, his prescribed route led through a neglected, ancient cathedral enclosed within the fortress. His fellow soldiers often laughed over the way he jogged through the castle when delivering the key, but he willingly suffered their jeers to get the ordeal over with as quickly as possible. More than once he offered to let another take his turn, but his chuckling comrades insisted that he perform the duty himself.

The weather that night was wretched. Hunched against the clammy, life-sapping chill radiating from the stone walls, the young soldier hastened along the passage. His teeth would have been chattering from cold if they hadn't been clenched so tightly in fear—the deserted old cathedral lay just ahead.

Trying his best to appear resolute and soldierly, he entered the ancient structure with his lantern held in front of him, like a magic talisman. Weird shadows, cast by the lantern's weak bubble of light, danced around the walls as he hurried down the silent aisle. He kept his eyes and his mind focused on the exit, a little doorway on the far wall. He was almost there.

He froze in his tracks. A huge dog crouched menacingly on the path, at the very edge of his lantern. It had the shaggy black coat of a spaniel, but it stood three times larger than any dog that ever had a human master. Its red eyes glinted back at the thunderstruck young man, reflecting the flickering light of his little lamp. It neither snarled nor growled, but its aura of cold foreboding made it more terrifying than an entire pack of mortal hounds.

The soldier's lantern shattered on the cathedral's flagstones. He turned and fled, screaming. His legs propelled him, by reflex and muscle memory, through the pitch-dark corridors of Peel Castle until he burst, howling, into the safety of the guardroom. White-faced, shaking, incoherent, he collapsed in front of the blazing fire.

"In God's name, man!" the sergeant shouted. "What's got into you? You only just left here!" The chattering guardsman could only mutter and stare, his breath coming in quick, ragged gasps. Someone thrust a bottle of strong whiskey into his shaking hands, and he drank deeply. At long last, he regained his senses.

Peel Castle, a former English stronghold off the Isle of Man, is the setting for the bizarre tale of the Moddey Dhoo.

"D-dog," he stammered, "b-black dog. In the ca-cathedral." In broken sentences and stuttered words, between frequent draughts of the powerful liquor, he managed to get his story out to the disbelieving soldiers. Although they had all heard stories of the Black Dogs, the older, more practical men weren't ready to accept the testimony of their superstitious young comrade.

"All right, all right," said one grizzled old veteran after the laughing and teasing had gone on a bit. "Come on, man. Let's go see this 'black dog' of yours and get that key up to the captain."

The young guard went white again, just as the color began to return to his cheeks. "No!" he cried. "I'm not going back down that passage! You can't make me go back there!"

"No?" the old guardsman asked, his eyebrow arching and his voice taking on a tone of menace. "Are you shirking your duty, soldier? Are you disobeying your orders?"

The frightened soldier stopped in mid-protest and stared up at the grim-faced veteran. The other guards looked on with malicious grins, clearly enjoying this little scene—such entertainment was rare on this godforsaken chunk of rock. The soldier shuddered, trapped between two wholly unpleasant options. Would he face the mystical threat of the thing in the passage or the physical threat of these military men?

The concrete promise of punishment proved more persuasive than the guardsman's fear, dimmed as it was by the whiskey. With one more good swig of the fiery liquor, the young man hauled himself to his unsteady feet, trying to keep his knees from shaking too badly.

"All right, then," he said, trying to muster a brave voice. "L-let's go."

This sparked more hearty laughter and mocking cheers from the gathered soldiers. "That's a boy, then! Go get 'im! Har har har!" "Aye! Put a leash on 'im and we'll teach him some tricks! Ha-ha!"

Leaving the noise and light of the warm guardroom, the young soldier and the veteran made their way down the passage. By this time, no doubt, the captain of the guard would be growing impatient. The damp cold of the fortress wrapped itself around them, chilling the older man and plunging the sweating younger man deeper into misery. He felt certain death or worse waited up ahead. The icy darkness mocked their guttering little candles as they came at last to the ancient cathedral.

The soldier could barely breathe as the older man led the way across the huge, shadow-filled hall. At last they came upon the shattered bits of the young guard's lantern and the scorchmarks left when the light's small reservoir of oil burned away on the stone floor.

The veteran poked at the shards with the toe of his boot, sending a cascade of high-pitched, tinkling echoes reverberating through the old cathedral. "I'm guessing this is where you saw your beastie, then?"

The young soldier looked frantically around, thrusting his inadequate little candle in all directions, searching for any sign of the enormous creature he'd seen not half an hour earlier. He saw nothing, just dust and the shattered fragments of the broken lantern.

"I…I saw it right here," he stammered, flushed with a strange combination of embarrassment and relief at the black dog's absence. "It was here! I swear I saw it, just as plainly as I see you now!"

"Aye, I don't doubt you, lad," the old soldier said, clapping the younger man on the shoulder. "A place like this, on a night like this, a man can get to seein' lots of things that aren't there. Pull yourself together and let's get this job done."

The bewildered young man-at-arms and his older companion completed their journey to the captain's quarters and returned to the guardroom without incident. Back in front of the bright, crackling fireplace, the young man could easily deflect or absorb the jibes of his fellow soldiers. He felt simply grateful and amazed to find himself alive after the night's ordeal.

As for his comrades, they wouldn't have laughed quite so heartily had they known that, soon enough, they too would meet the black dog.

The next day dawned in mist and cloud. The garrison of Peel Castle went through its unremarkable routine until the sun once again extinguished itself in the sea. As twilight fell, they closed and locked the castle gates as usual and lit the candles in the guardroom.

Just then, they heard the padding of heavy feet in the passageway. A huge black form emerged from the gloom of the doorway and stood in the flickering amber light from the candles.

The terrified men stood frozen in place as the fearsome creature stalked calmly into the room. When they thought back to the young guard's story from the previous night, the guards felt their neck hairs rise. They had mocked their friend, yet here the beast stood—a shaggy-haired spaniel, larger than any dog had a right to be. They gaped in silence as the dog padded softly across the room, yawned and lay down by the fire, its head resting on giant forepaws. Through luminous red eyes, it quietly watched them.

This time, it gave off no aura of terror. Instead, it seemed to radiate a sense of expectancy—of waiting, of watching and of warning. The armed men in the room far outnumbered the beast and certainly could have taken it, despite its size, had it been a natural animal. Nevertheless, not a single soldier considered taking up arms against it.

Gradually, as they realized that the dog posed no immediate threat to life or limb, the guards began to move and speak once more.

"Lord Almigh—" one guard began to whisper, but the sergeant cut him off with a sudden loud hiss.

"Shhhhhhhhh! You fool!" he shout-whispered in harsh tones. "Are you mad? Taking the Lord's name in vain in front of that thing! Don't you realize what it is?" The other shook his head.

"That thing," the sergeant continued, with the conviction of a prophet, "is obviously an evil spirit, sent by the Dev…uh, sent here to drag us down. It's just waiting for an excuse to take us. Do you all understand me?"

The men, all huddled against the far wall, nodded that they did. They surreptitiously tucked away their dice and stopped up their flasks. There would be no drinking or gambling that night.

"Good. And no profanity. Sure as I'm standing here, the first man who blasphemes in front of this thing will speak his next words in He…in a bad place."

Each man carefully guarded his tongue for fear that the creature would take exception.

One of the guardsmen then spoke up, more timidly than you'd expect from an experienced soldier. "Sir?" he called, almost squeaking. "What…what about the key, sir? I'd rather if…I mean, I'd rather not…"

"Hm? Oh, right," the sergeant responded. "It's your turn tonight, isn't it? Calm yourself, man." Based on the events of the previous night, he reasoned that the dog—the Moddey Dhoo he called it, Gaelic for "black dog"—only threatened solitary guards. From now on, he said, two men would transport the key together. At this suggestion, the fearful soldiers murmured their approval.

Of course, the sergeant's theory had yet to be tested. The two men chosen for the trip still felt understandably apprehensive. White-faced and trembling, they summoned what courage they could. They crept past the reclining dog, keeping as quiet and as far away as possible, and went out into the night.

The rest of the guards held their breath as they listened to the receding thump of boots on stone. The two candles faded into the distance, leaving the passage dark and silent once more. At that instant, the great dog silently raised itself up from the flagstones and, with another very dog-like yawn and stretch, padded off through the portal, melting into the shadows of the silent hallway.

Minutes felt like hours as the men waited for their comrades to return. Nobody dared speak; even a cough or the scrape of a chair earned sharp and reproachful glances. How long had they been gone? Ten minutes? Fifteen? Surely they should have returned by now.

The tension had become unbearable. "Maybe we ought to go see…" one soldier began. "Quiet!" said another, cutting him off. "Listen!"

They all cocked their ears toward the doorway. They heard the sound of heavy boots hurrying down the stone corridor and the jangle of weapons and gear as the two key bearers approached the guardroom. A moment later two very relieved men reentered the company of their fellow soldiers, who were almost as relieved as they.

One of the returning men looked over at where the dog had been. "Where did the creature go?" he asked.

"It followed you two down the passage soon after you'd gone," one of the others replied. "Didn't you see it? It must have been right behind you."

"If we'd seen it," responded the second courier, "I doubt we'd be standing here talking to you. We left and came back without seeing anyth…"

His words trailed off at the sight of his comrades' shocked expressions, their eyes focused on the passageway behind him. Turning, he saw what they saw: the Moddey Dhoo loomed in the doorway. It padded past the men and lay down to resume its fireside vigil, regarding the mystified soldiers through reflective red eyes.

"Well," said the sergeant, an exasperated tone of resignation in his voice, "if it doesn't want to leave, we'll just have to get used to it." His men could do nothing but agree. The unnatural beast seemed not to mean them any harm, provided they maintained the injunction against "profane" behavior. Perhaps the Moddey Dhoo would leave in its own time.

"Its own time," fittingly enough, turned out to be sunrise. The moment the sun crested the horizon, turning the swirling sea-mist of St. Patrick's Isle to the silver-gray of dawn, the soldiers' fireside guest rose from its resting place. Without so much as a baleful glance backward, it stalked off down the passageway that led to the old church. Somehow, though, the guardsmen knew they hadn't seen the last of their Moddey Dhoo. Sure enough, at sundown the enormous black spaniel emerged once more out of the shadowy hallway.

On this night three men escorted the key, since the captain himself had come to the guardroom to view the

Moddey Dhoo. Again, the dog followed the couriers when they left and reappeared after they returned (having left the amazed captain at his quarters). And again, when the sun rose, the dog disappeared into the cathedral passageway. Night after night the same ritual played out. Eventually, the guardsmen became used to the eerie dog's nightly presence.

Still, it wasn't the most soothing companion. The guards still regarded the dog as an evil presence, waiting for the opportunity to drag some soldier's soul to the devil. They didn't dare let slip a curse or a bit of profanity, and drinking and gambling were right out. They were a clean-spoken, well-behaved and bored group of military men. Something had to give.

Eventually, nine long nights after the young soldier first saw the black dog, something did. One of the guardsmen, known for his quick temper and boisterous ways, had devised a simple but elegant way around the sergeant's injunction against drinking during the night watch. He got drunk during the day and reported to the guardroom already halfway in the bag.

A thrill of panic ran through the soldiers as the drunkard stumbled into the guardroom, loudly (and badly) singing a particularly bawdy tavern song. The huge black spaniel seemed to become particularly alert to the noise.

"Have you lost your wits, man?" one of the others rasped. "What do you think you're playing at? You'll bring us all to ruin!"

This set the sodden soldier off. "Will I?" he shouted. "Will I? I'm sick of all this mousing around! I'm damned sick of it, and I'm damned sick of that damned dog!" He pointed squarely at the black spaniel by the fireplace. The other soldiers backed away from the drunk. The Moddey Dhoo just sat there, glaring at the shouting man.

"Give me that!" barked the drunk soldier, snatching the key from its appointed courier. "I'll find out!" he declared, as he grabbed up a candle and stormed into the dark corridor. "I'll find out if this Moddey Dhoo is a dog or a devil!" And with that, he disappeared into the shadows.

From a distance, his shouts still echoed through the passageway. All eyes turned to the Moddey Dhoo. To their horror, the fearsome beast picked itself up and bounded out of the room. The sounds of the raving man grew fainter until—silence.

Seconds crept by as the guards stared fearfully at one another in the sudden stillness. Maybe he's just gone out of earshot, they thought. Maybe he's gotten properly scared and shut himself up. Deep inside, though, they knew they were lying to themselves. Suddenly there rose from the cursed passageway—for that's what they now knew it to be—a sound like no other ever heard on earth.

It was a hellish blend of howl and scream, the rage of a beast and the terror of a man, blended with the roar of flames, the clash of metal and the grinding of stone. It tore through the chill air of Peel Castle, reverberating from wall to wall, wrapping hearts in cold fear. After what seemed like an eternity, the last horrible echoes fled away over the sea.

Long minutes passed. Finally, the men heard the very faintest of sounds coming from the dark passage—the scraping shuffle of human feet, the rattle of a soldier's gear, the muttering of a human voice. A tottering, wild-eyed figure came lurching out of the darkness. It was the drunkard, or what was left of him.

The guardsmen steered him to a chair in front of the fireplace, all asking at once, in a babble of fear, what had happened in that dread hallway.

"Am ma am ma ba ma ma maaaaaa," he murmured in reply. Slumped in the chair, he stared off mindlessly, as if gazing through the castle walls at something miles away.

"What? What's that? Get a grip on yourself," scolded one of the soldiers. Another soldier brought a flask of whiskey, but the amber liquid just dribbled from the man's slack lips and down his chin.

"He's gone mad from fear," the sergeant remarked. "Let's get him bedded down. Perhaps he'll recover by morning." As they hoisted the big man onto a bedroll, one of the guardsman made a surprising observation: the Moddey Dhoo had not returned.

Nor did it return the next night. All day they had questioned the stricken soldier, but he would not speak or make any other kind of intelligible communication. Prayers and blessings had no effect on his state, and he refused to take food, water or liquor. Neither would he sleep. The poor man could only stare into the distance and babble.

On the third night, they found him dead. He lay twisted in agony on his bedroll, his legs curled up and his arms splayed as though warding off an enemy. His eyes stared in fear, and his mouth gaped in a silent scream.

The Moddey Dhoo of Peel Castle, having taken its victim, was never seen again.

One additional wrinkle may shed some light, however dim, on this strange tale. In 1871, during an excavation under the ancient cathedral, workers unearthed the crypt of Simon, Bishop of Sodor and Man, who died in the year 1247. The skeleton of a dog lay curled up at the dead cleric's feet. Was this the Moddey Dhoo, or was it merely a weird coincidence?

Either way, the legend of the Moddey Dhoo lives on— an unforgettable chapter in the Isle of Man's great tradition of ghost stories.

The Treasure Dog of Lyme Regis

Throughout the world, Black Dogs serve numerous supernatural purposes. Some act as fearsome guardians, warning trespassers away from a certain area over the course of centuries. Others deliver omens of death and doom. Some seem relatively benign and do nothing other than leave people with a strange story to tell. Some actively steer wanderers away from disaster, and a few guide lucky people to caches of hidden treasure. The treasure dog of Lyme Regis, Dorset, was one such animal.

Our story begins in the 17th century, at a long-lost mansion known as Colway Manor. The master of Colway was an elderly, solitary man, the last survivor of a once-proud household. His only companion in the drafty confines of his rambling hermitage was his loyal little black dog. Every night, the two sat by the mansion's old fireplace, each in his own way silently contemplating the mysteries of life.

The old man's quiet retirement from the toils of the world was not destined to be peaceful, however; elderly men and women who choose to withdraw from the society of their fellows rarely escape their neighbors' often malicious whispers. In this case, the village rumor took the form of a simple equation. Item one: the inhabitants of Colway Manor had at one time been quite wealthy. Item two: the old man had modest expenses, keeping no servants and enjoying few luxuries. Conclusion: the master of Colway was obviously a miser, greedily hoarding his clan's fortune in his lonely manor house.

Inevitably, a pair of scoundrels caught wind of these rumored riches. They decided that they needed the gold more than any old hermit did.

The criminal duo barged into Colway late at night, just as the old man prepared to retire to bed. Laughing and jeering, they terrorized the poor man, savagely kicking his valiant but tiny dog down the stairs when it tried to defend its master. They ordered the master to reveal the location of his hidden treasures. When he refused, they began to beat him into submission. Perhaps they underestimated their victim's fragility, or perhaps they meant to kill him. Either way, the old man soon lay dead at their hands. As the thugs ransacked the place for valuables, the injured dog could do nothing but whine in grief at its master's side. It didn't stir from its sad vigil until it died, from exhaustion or starvation, a few days later.

The manor house lay abandoned until, during the English Civil War, it was almost completely destroyed. Only the large central hall and its huge stone fireplace survived more or less intact. Eventually, a farmer purchased the remnants of the mansion and converted it into a modest farmhouse.

After several uneventful decades, the house fell into the hands of a solitary old farmer. Like the former master of the manor, he loved to spend his evenings alone with his thoughts, beside the grand old fireplace. One night, though, a remarkable guest broke his solitude. A huge dog with eerie green eyes strode into the house and took up the seat opposite the startled farmer. There he remained until the old farmer, too frightened to get up and go to his bed, finally fell asleep where he sat. In the morning, he couldn't see the dog anywhere, nor could he find tracks in the damp ground outside.

For weeks, the unwelcome canine visitor disturbed the farmer's evening relaxation. Every time the poor man took his accustomed seat by the fire, the frightening dog materialized to join him. Eventually the farmer came to realize that the beast meant him no harm, and he came to accept and even enjoy the company of his new friend. His neighbors, on the other hand, urged him to drive the dog away. For the good of his immortal soul, they said, he had best be rid of the unholy creature.

"And why should I drive him away?" the farmer replied. "He's quiet, he doesn't eat my food and doesn't bother me or anyone else. Of all the creatures on this farm, he's the easiest and cheapest to keep!"

Unfortunately, the old man's good sense couldn't sway his gossipy and superstitious neighbors. Some shunned him outright, while others teased him for lacking the courage to rid himself of the black dog. One night, the farmer found himself at the pub among a group of these so-called friends. As the ale flowed, so did the mockery. The jokes came hard and fast.

Finally, he could take it no longer. Drunk and infuriated, he stormed out of the public house and returned home, determined at last to drive the dog away. He found the dog waiting for him, as usual, by the hearth. The farmer snatched up an iron fire poker and brandished it angrily at the apparition.

"Get out of here!" he yelled, taking wild, drunken swings with the heavy implement. "Get out of my house you devil! Begone!" The poker clanged against the stone chimney, striking sparks and sending chips flying, but the dog scampered nimbly out of the way and fled up the ladderlike steps to the attic.

"You're not getting away from me, you beast!" raved the intoxicated old man. He clambered awkwardly up the stairs, still carrying his improvised weapon in one hand. "There ain't no other way down from there! I'll have you out of my house!"

As he entered the nearly pitch-dark attic, the farmer saw the black dog watching him from the opposite side, its great eyes shining green. The old man advanced on the dog warily and somewhat unsteadily, until he came within striking range. Then he rushed at the beast with a great shout, swinging the poker like a broadsword.

Back in the 17th century, the ghost dog of Lyme Regis helped an old man discover hidden riches.

Once again, the poker merely whistled harmlessly through thin air. The dog had leaped out of the way and escaped—straight through the solid wood and thatch of the roof. Astounded, drunk and flat on his backside from the force of his missed blow, the thwarted man again lashed out wildly, striking the roof at the point where the black dog had vanished.

With a hollow crack, the wood gave way. From a concealed space in the ceiling, a large old box thudded heavily on the floor at the old man's feet.

The farmer dropped his poker with a clatter. He crouched down to open the box, his heart pounding with curiosity. Even in the attic's dim light, he could clearly see the gleam of silver and gold coins, dating back to the reign of Charles I.

The old man recalled the half-forgotten story of the master of Colway and his loyal dog. Could this be the unfortunate man's hidden cache of treasure? And could the black beast have been the apparition of his canine companion?

Apparently, the farmer decided that this must be the case. He took his sudden miraculous wealth, constructed a new public house and named it the Black Dog Inn.

But the treasure dog of Lyme Regis didn't completely disappear from the scene. Over the years, pet dogs often mysteriously disappeared in the narrow alley adjacent to the Black Dog Inn. People blamed a mysterious apparition—"a black, shaggy dog with fiery eyes…the size of a young calf," as one 19th-century witness described it. Accordingly, the road earned the name "Dog Lane."

An inn still stands on the same spot today. The building is newer, but the name—the Old Black Dog Guest House— preserves the old legend. Local pet owners remember the legend as well, never letting their beloved pooches wander too near the narrow confines of Dog Lane.

The Death Dog
of Newgate Prison

These same men, day by day, and hour by hour, pass and repass this gloomy depository of the guilt and misery of London, in one perpetual stream of life and bustle...not even knowing, or if they do, not heeding, the fact that as they pass one particular angle of the massive wall with a light laugh or a merry whistle, they stand within one yard of a fellow-creature, bound and helpless, whose hours are numbered, from whom the last feeble ray of hope has fled for ever, and whose miserable career will shortly terminate in a violent and shameful death.

—Charles Dickens, "A Visit to Newgate," 1836

For centuries before its demolition in 1903, Newgate Prison ranked among London's most notorious and chilling landmarks. A monument to the savage medieval justice of England's unreformed penal system, the prison earned a reputation for brutality, deprivation, disease and death. For over 1000 years a prison had stood on that site. It was a nexus of misery in the heart of London, haunted, they say, by the "black dog."

The phrase "Black Dogs of Newgate" holds different meaning for different people. Some see it as a metaphor for the savage conditions that existed within the prison's walls and for the despair and hopelessness it brought to the souls of both men and women (at any one time, Newgate's women's section housed hundreds of prisoners). Some people use the term "black dogs" to describe the brutal wardens and guards who ruled Newgate with fear and force. "Making the black dog walk" was also prison slang for the violent and humiliating hazing that all new prisoners were forced to endure.

Finally, there is the more literal Black Dog of Newgate. For hundreds of years, a dark and silent hound reportedly appeared whenever a condemned prisoner made the long walk to the gallows. Some say it still haunts the vicinity of the long-gone prison.

As London's main prison, Newgate housed the condemned while they awaited execution. The cold, damp prison was often packed to the walls with unfortunates, because at the time the death penalty extended beyond traitors and murderers. Great numbers of debtors, fraud artists, burglars, arsonists, highwaymen and others met their death at the end of a Newgate rope.

This suited the masses of London well. From 1783 until 1868, when the practice was abolished, public executions outside Newgate provided the city's most popular entertainment. Every Monday morning, the crowds thronged to the street. Wealthy and influential individuals bribed or intimidated their way into the best viewing locations, to jeer the condemned on their walk to the gallows. In the midst of this bloodthirsty circus, they say, the Black Dog would appear.

Accounts of the Black Dog vary widely. Some described the beast as a seemingly ordinary dog, apart from its mysterious arrival and departure. It would appear at the side of

Although its origins remain a mystery, the Black Dog of Newgate Prison continued to appear long after public executions ceased.

a doomed soul as he or she walked through the howling crowd to the waiting rope. Others saw the dog as a shape-less, ghostly shadow that flickered across the walls and paving stones during the prisoners' last walks. Long after public hangings were stopped, people continued to see this strange, doglike spirit on execution mornings.

People also offer wildly differing theories on the Black Dog's origins. Some insist that it's the ghost of a hanged highwayman, imagined into animal shape by observers familiar with folktales of sinister black dogs. Others believe that an ancient nature spirit became trapped by the negative energy generated by Newgate's centuries of misery and death.

A 17th-century booklet puts forward an even more fantastic tale. A highwayman by the name of Hutton turned to literature while awaiting execution in Newgate (his other known works include a long poem warning young people of the horrible fate that waits at the end of a life of crime). Hutton's tract, entitled *The Black Dog of Newgate Gaol,* supposedly tells of events hundreds of years earlier, in the 13th century, when conditions were even worse.

In this account, the prisoners of Newgate—plagued by vermin, disease and violence—are being starved by pitiless jailers who hoard the inmates' meager rations for themselves. Driven mad by deprivation and hunger, the prisoners resort to cannibalism, with the relatively strong preying on the weak. One of these victims was a scholarly man, with more than a little knowledge of black magic and sorcery. Soon after this wizard had been butchered and eaten by his hunger-crazed fellow inmates, the elusive Black Dog began stalking the ancient prison, appearing whenever another condemned soul met its violent fate.

Although the old prison was demolished long ago, along with the cruel system of institutional violence it represented, some say the Black Dog still lingers in its old haunt. People often glimpse strange shadows in the alleys and courtyards near the old prison site, weird doglike shapes that radiate an aura of sadness and despair.

One location, Amen Court, lies close to both the prisoners' final walkway and to the prison graveyard. It has a reputation as the area's most haunted spot. Experts say that Jack Sheppard, a prisoner who escaped Newgate three times before finally being executed, vies with the Black Dog for the right to haunt the centuries-old courtyard. Unfortunately, Amen Court lies on private property. It's attached to nearby St. Paul's Cathedral, and the administrators don't encourage visits by curious ghost seekers.

Doom Dog of
the Hanging Hills

Around the world, people fear Black Dog apparitions as bad omens—portents of tragedy for those unlucky enough to encounter them. They say that a brush in the night with one of these glowering, red-eyed shadow dogs dooms someone to imminent accidental death or serious illness.

American ghost lore has more than its share of these dogs of death, but not all of them take the form of growling, wolf-sized beasts. One of them—the Doom Dog of the Hanging Hills—appears as a playful, friendly pup.

The Hanging Hills, the remains of ancient lava flows, rise to 1000 feet above sea level and "hang" above the old silver town of Meriden, Connecticut. Every year, thousands of hikers enjoy the area's panoramic views and lush high-altitude forests. Geologists flock there as well, drawn by the endless treasure trove of strange rock formations and rich mineral deposits.

But it's a place of tragedy as well as beauty. Places such as Lamentation Mountain and Misery Brook stand as memorials to the prospectors and hikers who have perished on the rugged pathways. The Hanging Hills offer many challenging hiking routes, and even the mildest carries the threat of a long fall down the face of an eons-old basalt cliff. Local legend says that the Doom Dog warns luckless hikers of this fate—or, perhaps, leads them to it.

Researchers say the dog's appearances come in threes, as is the case with many death omens. The first time he appears is for joy. The second time is for sorrow. The third and final time is for death.

Many unknowing hikers have returned from a ramble in the hills, talking about the good-natured little dog they befriended on the trail. They cut their stories short, though, when they see the look of terror on the townsfolks' suddenly pale faces. The locals know better than to take such sightings lightly. When people see the dog, they often end up dead in the hills.

Of course, not everyone heeds the warnings. One who didn't, a New York geologist named W.H.C. Pynchon, provided a detailed account of his encounters with the Doom Dog of the Hanging Hills. In the spring 1889 issue of the *Connecticut Quarterly*, he told of the first and second times he met the animal. He never had the opportunity to describe the third.

Once for joy...

On a fine morning, the young geologist ventured out into the Hanging Hills to gather and study rare rock specimens. As he guided his small horse-drawn wagon down the rough road that skirts Lake Merimere, Pynchon spotted a particularly interesting rock formation: a huge, gnarled outcrop of gray stone. As he lighted from his cart to study the rocks more closely, a dark little dog—possibly some type of spaniel or terrier—scampered down from the boulders to greet him. When Pynchon continued his journey, the spirited but oddly silent canine trotted along beside the wagon.

On such a beautiful spring morning, amid such unspoiled beauty, Pynchon was happy to have such a quiet and agreeable traveling companion. When they reached the town of Southington, Pynchon stopped for lunch at a local tavern. Returning to his wagon after a relaxed meal, he was surprised to find the little dog still sitting expectantly beside the wagon. The dog followed the buggy down the winding track towards Meriden until they reached the weird outcropping where they first met. At that point, Pynchon looked over his shoulder to check on his companion, and barely caught a glimpse of the small, dark form scampering soundlessly into the forest.

...twice for sorrow...

A few years later, Pynchon returned to the hills whose beauty and scientific value had so impressed him. This time, he brought along a human companion, a fellow geologist who had already made many similar study excursions to the Hanging Hills.

The night before heading into the back country, the pair swapped stories around the fireplace. Pynchon's friend mentioned that a friendly little black dog had twice accompanied him on previous trips. He and Pynchon had both heard the local legend of the Doom Dog, of course, but they were rugged and practical field geologists—men of science. They had no time for ominous folktales and backward superstitions. In good spirits, they eventually said their goodnights and hit the hay.

The next morning dawned bright and clear, but blustery and cold even by the standards of a Connecticut February. It wasn't the best weather for climbing but, like many in their profession, the two geologists were competent mountaineers. They set out for West Peak with confidence.

They chose a route of ascent through a gap between two towering cliffs. The winter wind lashed Pynchon's face as he struggled up the snow-encrusted stones. As he looked up at the twin black spires of ancient lava, he found the words of the 23rd Psalm running unbidden through his mind: "Yea, though I walk through the valley of the shadow of death…"

Pynchon soon forgot his melancholy mood, absorbed in the rigors of the challenging climb. Nearing the top of West Peak, they stopped for a brief rest before the final push to the summit. Suddenly, unbelievably, the men spotted the small black dog sitting on a ledge above them. The little mutt wagged its tail and barked at them, silently as ever.

In their haste to meet their old friend, the two veteran climbers became careless. Pynchon's companion lost his

Did a mysterious spirit dog lure hikers to their deaths in the Hanging Hills of Connecticut?

footing on the ice-covered stone slope. Pynchon scrambled to save him but could only watch helplessly as his friend tumbled like a rag doll down the cliff face, his body landing twisted and broken on the jagged rocks below.

  ...thrice for death.

After publishing this account and witnessing his friend's tragic fate, you would think Pynchon would have steered clear of the Doom Dog's territory. Alas, such was not the case. He found himself irresistibly drawn back to the black Hanging Hills, compelled to retrace the route of that last, fatal climb.

By this time, the locals had come to know and like the big-city outsider. They begged him not to go into the hills. After all, he had seen the Doom Dog twice; a third encounter, they argued, would mean certain death. Ever the pragmatic scientist, Pynchon refused to be deterred, and set out for West Peak on yet another cold, clear winter morning. Later that day, searchers found his shattered body at almost the exact spot where his friend had died years before.

Had Pynchon made one final rendezvous with his canine companion? No one can say for sure, but in Meriden they consider it a certainty. Why, though, had the geologist returned so single-mindedly to West Peak, after having seen the black dog's curse in action? Had he simply allowed his scientific zeal and rational skepticism to over-rule his fear?

The reason may be more sinister than that. In Meriden, some say that the little black dog is more than just an omen or warning—it's an inescapable curse. If you see the dog, even once, your fate is sealed. One way or another, you'll return for your portion of sorrow and your dose of death. Pynchon, his friend and dozens of others who have myste-riously fallen to their deaths were doomed from the moment they first made friends with that affectionate little black dog in the rugged rocks of the Hanging Hills.

3
Animal
Spirits
of
American
History

Old Raridan

Lake White State Park, in the picturesque wooded hills of Ohio's Pike County, seems the perfect place for a peaceful getaway. But looks can be deceiving. If you venture out on a moonless night, when the west wind howls between the ridges, you just might cross paths with the restless spirit of Old Raridan, last and greatest of Ohio's long-gone wolf pack.

Perhaps you're familiar with the phenomenon of "animal graveyards," where wild animals, for unknown and mysterious reasons, go to die. Pike County was home to one such spot. For centuries, the area's old, sick or injured gray wolves crawled off to die at the flat top of a towering granite hill.

The hill earned the name "Great Buzzard's Rock" after the flocks of vultures that gathered there in the pursuit of an easy meal. It later became known as "Big Rock," the hill's current name, but the friendlier title didn't stop the wolves from making their last journey up its sides.

Before the arrival of white settlers, the Shawnee and the prehistoric Adena and Hopewell tribes coexisted with the wolves and respected Big Rock as a site of spiritual power. But beginning in the late 18th century, white men began to push into the Ohio Valley. Revolutionary War veterans claimed homesteads in payment for their military service, and the coexistence between man and wolf ended forever.

Even the most powerful wolf is no match for a determined frontiersman with a gun. As area farmers mercilessly hunted the wolves that preyed on their livestock, wolf bones began to pile up on Big Rock. The hill's buzzards grew so fat they could barely fly, and the wolves were driven to the brink of extinction.

However, two wolves refused to die as easily as their brothers and sisters. Night after night the huge and ancient Old Raridan and his mate raided the homesteads, and night after night they escaped into the woods. The last wolves in the area, they eluded all attempts to bring them down. The settlers grew terrified by the very thought of this seemingly unkillable wolf and his mate. Old Raridan had supernatural powers, they said. He was a demon, a werewolf. Local ministers went so far as to say prayers of exorcism.

One day, though, Old Raridan finally met his match. A large group of heavily armed hunters, a posse that would do even the most notorious human desperado proud, cornered Old Raridan's mate against the steep face of Big Rock. They unleashed a withering barrage of shot, and the female fell. When the hunters loosed their dogs to finish her off, Old Raridan burst into the clearing with a blood-curdling howl. The hunters opened fire again, but the mortally wounded old wolf continued to fight savagely. Eventually, the hunters called off their dogs and fell back to observe Old Raridan's last breaths.

The amazed homesteaders then witnessed a testament to Old Raridan's fidelity and willpower. Broken and bleeding, he limped to his companion's side, gripped her lifeless body with his powerful jaws and slowly dragged her up the slope of Big Rock. Reaching the summit, where so many of his kind had gone to their rest, Old

Many visitors to Lake White State Park in Ohio have heard the bone-chilling howl of Old Raridan, a legendary ghost wolf.

Raridan gently laid his mate down. He then turned his head to the sky, and with his final breath emitted a monstrous howl that echoed through the hills.

But did his powerful spirit pass on? Soon after Old Raridan died on Big Rock, people of the area began to report hearing the loud, bone-chilling cry of a wolf in the night. To this day, campers and hikers are often terrified by this heartbreaking howl. The locals say it's the ghost of Old Raridan, guarding over his race's ancient graveyard.

In death, as in life, the elusive Old Raridan is far more likely to be heard than seen. If you're attentive, though, you might catch a flash of gray in the trees, a pair of yellow eyes in the night or a four-footed silver shadow far too large to be a dog.

These days, as we sit safe under electric lights and without wolves at the door, the memory of Old Raridan has faded somewhat. But his legend stands as a reminder of the mystery and power of the wilderness.

The Ghost Horses of Palo Duro Canyon

The beautiful Palo Duro Canyon in the Texas Panhandle embodies the stereotypical "Western" landscape. It seems to invite myths and legends. Lost gold mines, hoarding their secret and glittering riches, lie hidden in the canyon's twists and turns. Mexican desperadoes, frontier lawmen and lone cowboys ride through the night, reenacting their past adventures. And on moonlit evenings, they say, one can sometimes hear the thundering hoofbeats of a thousand horses running free—the tragic Ghost Herd of Palo Duro Canyon.

Sometimes called "the Grand Canyon of Texas," the Palo Duro ranks among the earth's most magical places. Carved out over the eons by wind, weather and the winding waters of the Red River, it stretches 120 miles long and in places 20 miles wide. Improbable spires of stone soar hundreds of feet into the huge skies, and vast eroded walls of ancient rock reveal layer upon layer of our planet's history.

Against this unimaginably ancient backdrop, human history in the Palo Duro seems painfully brief—the blink of an eye. It began a mere 12,000 years ago, when ancient nomadic hunters stalked now-extinct game, mammoths and giant bison in the area. Much later, the Apache claimed the canyon, only to be displaced in their own time by the Kiowa and Comanche. In 1874, they too lost the land following a series of battles and skirmishes that came to be known as the Red River War.

The seeds of the war were sown when the federal government failed to make good on its obligations under the 1867 Treaty of Medicine Lodge. Promised shipments of rations and supplies either came up short or failed to arrive at all. Pledges of law enforcement, to stop the illicit and socially destructive trade in liquor and booze by white traffickers, were likewise abandoned. White cattle rustlers and horse thieves who raided Native territory were seldom caught because they were seldom pursued; when they were caught, they were seldom punished.

The two Indian agents in the area at the time, Quaker missionaries named John Miles and James Haworth, did their best to deal with the situation, but the military and the Office of Indian Affairs offered little help. Treaty articles prohibited white encroachment on Indian lands, but between 1872 and 1874 large parties of ruthless and well-organized hunters completely wiped out the buffalo herds on the Cheyenne-Arapaho reservation. The army merely looked on.

Soon after 1000 Kiowa horses were slaughtered during the Red River War, a ghostly herd began to rumble through Palo Duro Canyon.

Their livelihood gone, their very identity stolen, some Comanche vowed revenge. A large war party headed west to the buffalo hunters' camp, at Adobe Walls on the Canadian River. Seven hundred Comanche, Kiowa, Cheyenne and Arapaho laid siege to the encampment between June 27 and July 1, 1874, leaving 3 whites dead and up to 70 Indian warriors dead or wounded. The Battle of Adobe Walls triggered a summer-long series of bloody skirmishes, battles and pursuits. Eventually, the army adopted a strategy of total suppression and removal. They drove the Natives back into the canyons, their traditional safe haven, to be either subdued or annihilated.

By late September, the warriors and their families were holed up in Palo Duro Canyon, guided by the Kiowa shaman Maman-ti.

On September 28, the Fourth U.S. Cavalry, led by Colonel Ranald S. Mackenzie, plus a number of Tonkawa scouts led by Chief Johnson, launched a surprise attack. Comanche leader Red Warbonnet spotted the soldiers and fired a warning shot before being killed by the Tonkawas. However, the Natives, their villages scattered around the canyon, could not mount a unified defense.

First, Mackenzie destroyed Red Warbonnet's village and allowed the Tonkawas to loot it. Panic quickly spread among the other villages, and groups of people began to scramble desperately out of the canyon. Scattered defensive sniping did little to deter Mackenzie's men, and by the time the sun went down the battle was over. The warriors had been driven out and their possessions, including most of their winter food supply, captured. The demoralized survivors—only three warriors were killed in the battle—straggled back to the reservation. The last armed Indian resistance against the whites had ended.

The defeated warriors left the canyon on foot. Colonel Mackenzie's most critical blow was the capture of some 1400 Kiowa horses. Magnificent beasts, strong and loyal, they had given the warriors their only hope of matching the U.S. army's mobility and military strength. With the horses gone, they would not be able to hunt or travel over long distances, and their fates would lie at the mercy of white administration.

Recognizing this, Mackenzie took steps to ensure that the warriors could never again use their horses. After letting Tonkawa Chief Johnson choose 400 of the animals as a further spoil of war, he ordered his soldiers to slaughter the rest of the herd on the spot.

Records tell of soldiers turning away, retching at the massacre they were forced to carry out. Over 1000 horses died screaming on the canyon floor. Since then, the doomed herd has haunted the red rocks of Palo Duro.

Years later, an English professor at West Texas A&M University invited a Kiowa chief from New Mexico to speak to her Native American Literature class. The chief readily accepted, not only for the opportunity to broaden cultural understanding, but also for the chance to visit several of his people's most sacred sites.

Under clear fall skies and a bright Texas full moon, the professor drove the chief to the south end of Palo Duro Canyon State Park. They stood at the historical marker commemorating Colonel Mackenzie's rout and read the park's concise and businesslike description. After a few minutes, the Kiowa chief turned and slowly walked out onto the ancient battlefield.

The professor followed at a respectful distance, not speaking, barely even breathing. The chief, surrounded by the ghosts of his ancestors, began to weep quietly. Finally gathering himself together, he began to chant and pray, singing ancient songs of mourning. As his strong voice cut through the clear night, the professor found herself moved to tears as well.

Soon, she heard a faint rumble in the distance, like thunder from a far-off storm—but there was no storm on this cloudless night. The chief heard the sound too and stopped his chanting. The thundering grew louder, and nearer, until they both recognized it as the sound of a massive stampede of horses. They wheeled around, looking for the source.

There, on the rim of the canyon, they saw a herd of indistinct, shifting shadows in the moonlight. The pounding hoofbeats died down to a patter as the phantom horses looked down into the canyon, agitated and nervous. They seemed to be searching for the departed masters who had summoned them to the spot.

The chief and the professor, strangely unafraid, looked up at them in awe. After a long moment of silent regard, the ghostly shapes on the canyon rim receded. The sound of running horses rose again, then faded back into the night, leaving Palo Duro Canyon once again empty and silent.

The Red Ghost

It can seem like the hills and deserts of the American Southwest are populated more by ghosts than people. The shades of prospectors, desperadoes and wronged women haunt the ghost towns and wastelands they walked in life.

Animal ghosts are common here, too. Spectral horses thunder through moonlit canyons, and phantom dogs, loyal even beyond death, stand guard over long-forgotten claims. But the most unusual creature of all is the Red Ghost—a huge, crimson camel that gallops through old Nevada silver-mining country, its last unfortunate rider still lashed in the saddle.

You might have a hard time picturing a camel in Nevada, but these "ships of the desert" have a long, strange history in the region. In the 1850s, the U.S. Army's responsibilities increased after the discovery of gold in California. This posed a problem: how to resupply far-flung outposts across the harsh terrain. A young lieutenant named George Grossman thought of a solution. He lobbied the army to adopt desert-bred camels as pack animals and mounts. In 1855, with the support of Senator Jefferson Davis, Congress approved $30,000 for Grossman's plan. The army imported an initial herd of over 30 camels from Arabia.

Technically, the camels perfectly suited the hot plains and rocky passes of the Southwest. Fast, sure-footed and immensely strong, they outperformed horses and oxen in nearly every way. After trekking with 25 camels from El Paso to California, Lieutenant Edward Beale reported that "the harder the test they are put to, the more fully they seem to justify all that can be said of them. They pack water for days under a hot sun and never get a drop; they pack heavy burdens of corn and oats for months and never get a grain; and on the bitter greasewood and other worthless shrubs, not only subsist, but keep fat."

Despite their advantages, however, camels proved difficult to integrate. They're intelligent and moody and don't get along well with other animals. They also suffer from an image problem. The proud soldiers and frontiersmen of the young nation just couldn't see themselves swaying along on the backs of these ugly, smelly, foreign beasts.

When the Civil War broke out in 1861, the army could no longer afford experimental programs that didn't contribute to the war effort. Within a few years, they disbanded the Camel Corps, selling some of the animals and releasing the rest into the wild.

The region's Natives hunted the camels for meat, and a truly viable wild camel population never emerged. Nevertheless, the remnants of the Camel Corps and their offspring lingered well into the 20th century, providing the basis for numerous "ghost camel" yarns.

In 1883, a young woman was found savagely trampled to death on Eagle Creek Ranch, Arizona. Strange hoofprints, twice the size of a horse's, surrounded her mangled body, and clumps of matted red hair hung from nearby thorn bushes. Two nights later, a miner awoke to discover an unknown creature rampaging through his camp. He ran into a nearby town screaming about a "red demon," and when he returned to camp he too found hoofprints and coarse red hair. As the sightings continued, it became

The Red Ghost, the spirit of a camel left over from the U.S. Army's long-defunct Camel Corps, still materializes near Virginia City, Nevada.

clear that the "demon" was in fact an unusually large camel.

The story became even weirder a few years later. A rancher got a good long look at what was then known as the Red Ghost, and he reported that the creature carried a rider, apparently dead. Soon after, a pair of prospectors spotted the ghost and thought they saw something fall off its back. When they investigated, they found a human skull lying on the ground.

The Red Ghost and its now headless rider continued to appear across Arizona and Nevada until one day in 1893, when a farmer named Hastings saw a huge red creature rummaging through his turnip patch. Aiming his trusty buffalo gun from the safety of his kitchen, Hastings brought the beast down with a single shot. He took one look at the shaggy corpse, a headless human skeleton lashed in its saddle, and knew that he had killed the Red Ghost.

The cadaver was so tightly bound to the camel—tied there, some said, by Native Americans as a grim warning to would-be trespassers—that the leather straps had cut deep into the animal's flanks, leaving terrible scars and continually opening new wounds. The ongoing agony must have driven the poor creature to its violent rampages. Clearly Hastings' shot had been an act of mercy.

Although its earthly pain had ended, the Red Ghost was denied rest. To this day, people in the area sometimes see a large camel, speeding its grisly cargo through the desert night.

Fittingly, the Red Ghost's favorite haunting ground is the old Nevada silver mining town of Virginia City, home of the annual Virginia City Camel Races. The races, commemorating the history of the U.S. Army Camel Corps, attract thousands of tourists every year.

If you're ever in Virginia City during a full moon, look up at the slopes of Sun Mountain, high above the town. You just might spot a majestic red camel with a skeletal rider—an eerie reminder of one of the most unusual chapters in the history of the West.

Lincoln's Funeral Horses

A lonesome train on a lonesome track—
Seven coaches painted black—
A slow train, a quiet train
Carrying Lincoln home again
— Millard Lampell, "The Lonesome Train"

For nearly 140 years, along the rail lines curving from Baltimore to Albany and Columbus to Springfield, witnesses have reported an eerie, haunting apparition. A ghostly steam train rolls along at funeral speed, draped in the black garlands of mourning, its whistle moaning long and low. And in the towns en route, people often see a phantom team of wraithlike horses drawing an ornate hearse wagon slowly along the main thoroughfare. The sight, they say, exudes an aura of unbearable tragedy and grief.

Whose body lies within that stately wagon? Whose death has been so majestically mourned by ghosts for nearly a century and a half? It is, of course, President Abraham Lincoln. In the spring of 1865, his funeral procession made its way from Washington to a tomb in Springfield, Illinois, retracing in reverse the route Lincoln took to Washington as president-elect in 1861. Every spring since then, the phantom train repeats its somber journey.

The specter of President Lincoln looms large in American ghost lore, his reputed haunts far outnumbering those of any other historical figure. From famous locations such as the White House and Gettysburg, to countless hotels and inns across the country, virtually every place the 16th president spoke, slept or ate has its own story of "Lincoln's ghost." This seems only fitting, as Lincoln was among history's most mystically and spiritually attuned presidents.

Lincoln made no secret of his spiritualist beliefs. For example, he remarked in a letter to a friend that he had always carried "a strong tendency towards mysticism" and that he felt guided by a power from above. The death of his son Willie in 1862 only deepened his convictions. He became fascinated with spirit communication, holding séances in the White House in an attempt to contact the spirit of his beloved boy.

Lincoln also experienced seemingly prophetic dreams and visions. On April 4, 1865, he described one of these in in his journal:

> After I retired I soon began to dream. There seemed to be a deathlike stillness about me. Then I heard subdued sobs, as if a number of people were weeping. I thought I left my bed and wandered downstairs. There the silence was broken by the same pitiful sobs, but the mourners were invisible. I went from room to room; no living person was in sight, but the same mournful sounds of distress met me as I passed along.
>
> Determined to find the cause of the state of things so mysterious and so shocking, I kept on until I arrived at the East Room, which I entered.

Before me was a catafalque, on which rested a corpse wrapped in funeral vestments. Around it were stationed soldiers who were acting as guards, and there were a throng of people, some gazing mournfully upon the corpse, whose face was covered; others were weeping pitifully.

"Who is dead in the White House?" I demanded of one of the soldiers. "The president," was his answer. "He was killed by an assassin." Then came a loud burst of grief from the crowd, which awoke me from my dream. I slept no more that night; and although it was only a dream, I have been strangely annoyed by it ever since.

Ten days later, President Lincoln was dead by an assassin's bullet. On April 21 the black-draped train left Washington, bearing Lincoln's casket and the tiny coffin of Willie, who had been disinterred to be reburied beside his father. At stops along the train's 1654-mile journey, teams of magnificent white horses drew the hearse through the crowded streets, allowing shocked and grieving Americans to mourn their slain leader.

And mourn they did, in an outpouring of public grief unmatched before or since. On April 23 in Philadelphia, an estimated 300,000 mourners filed past the president's coffin. Two days later in New York, 75,000 citizens marched in the funeral procession. Hundreds of thousands of others crowded the route, and some spent up to $100 each to rent windows with good views. Similar scenes played out at each of the train's stops. Finally, on an

The spirit steeds from President Lincoln's funeral train arouse a deep sense of loss in those who encounter them.

unusually hot May 4 in Springfield, the body of Abraham Lincoln was laid to rest.

The very next spring, witnesses began to report seeing ghostly images of President Lincoln's funeral procession in the streets along the funeral route. In the decades since, dozens of others have seen it as well.

The apparition takes widely varied forms. Some witnesses describe the horses as faint, black-draped wraiths. For others, the splendid white team and elaborate hearse appear exactly as they did in life. Still others see terrifying, skeletal horses, their blankets in tatters. And some don't see the horses at all, but hear the clopping of hooves and the creak of wheels as the procession passes by. Almost always, however, the funeral train fills witnesses with an overwhelming sensation of deep grief.

Rick Miller (not his real name), a retired businessman from Cleveland, describes his encounter with Lincoln's hearse as "more like a sudden flash of memory than what I imagined seeing a ghost would be like." Late one April night in the mid-'70s, Miller, unable to sleep, decided to take an aimless drive around town. A wave of sadness suddenly overcame him, forcing him to pull his car over.

"I couldn't keep driving," he recalls. "It was this blast of sadness and loss mixed with shock. I was numb, almost paralyzed—I could barely see the road. I nearly started crying right there."

The initial "blast" of emotion passed, but the inexplicable grief remained. Miller had to get out of the car to catch his breath. Then, looking up the street, he saw a team of white horses, draped in dark blankets, pulling a large, ornate hearse. He knew right away that he wasn't looking at a real horse team on the streets of Cleveland. In fact, he says, "It wasn't like seeing at all. It felt more like remembering, or déjà vu—like when you pass a place where something good or bad happened to you, and you can't help but picture it." After about 30 seconds, the horses with their grim cargo—and the overwhelming aura of grief that surrounded them—disappeared.

Miller now feels certain he witnessed Abraham Lincoln's horse-drawn hearse. On April 28, 1865, the funeral procession carried the slain president's body from Cleveland's Union Station to its viewing location in Monument Square. Over the course of 15 hours, 150,000 mourners filed past the coffin.

Many people believe that ghostly apparitions are "residual fields." When people experience deeply emotional events, their minds can leave behind a kind of spiritual residue, to be replayed later in the minds of witnesses. What could be more emotional than the grief of an entire city, of an entire nation, as it watched a team of brilliant white horses carry a beloved president to his grave?

The Demon Cat of Capitol Hill

The U.S. Capitol in Washington, D.C., has a reputation as one of the world's most haunted buildings. Presidents, lawmakers, soldiers, heroes, villains and ordinary folk by the dozen spend their afterlives in the heart of American democracy. They wander the Capitol's marble corridors, chambers and galleries, from the great Rotunda to the most obscure back stairwell. At least one animal spirit keeps these human ghosts company: the Demon Cat of Capitol Hill.

Over the years, the vaults and passageways underneath the Capitol have periodically been overrun by mice and rats. At one point in the late 1800s, the situation got so bad that the staff released large numbers of domestic cats into the basement levels. Once things were back under control, they rounded up the mousers and gave them to good homes.

Of course, this was no easy task. People often use the phrase "like herding cats" to describe an impossible organizational challenge. Inevitably, the staff left behind at

The U.S. Capitol in Washington, D.C., is haunted by the so-called Demon Cat of Capitol Hill.

least one rat catcher. Over a century later, it still prowls the subterranean halls.

The apparition, later known as the Demon Cat, made its first appearance sometime in the early 1920s. A security officer, on routine night patrol through a long, dimly lit corridor, spotted a small black cat walking toward him. From a distance, the animal seemed perfectly friendly. As it approached, though, its purr became a yowl. It raised its hackles and bared its needle-sharp

The cat is said to patrol the halls during national crises or right before a new president is inaugurated.

fangs. Worst of all, it increased in size with every step, until it had transformed into a huge panther. Snarling, it pounced at the petrified guard.

Just as the feral predator was about to crush the screaming guard to the ground, slicing into him with claws and teeth, it vanished. The poor patrolman stood there trembling, terrified almost to death but physically unhurt.

Since then, numerous guards and Capitol employees have encountered a mysterious, angry cat in the grand old building's underground maze. Each time, the snarling black cat grows angrier and more hostile, but it invariably vanishes without a trace. According to legend, the Demon Cat appears most often at times of great national crisis, or before a change of presidency.

To this day, visitors to the Small Senate Rotunda can see a set of mysterious pawprints embedded in the stone floor. Proof of an otherworldly feline? Well, not necessarily. Apparently, a gas explosion in the 1880s damaged the original marble flagstones. Repairmen poured concrete in their place, and one of the Capitol cats must have walked across it before it had set.

That's the official explanation, anyway.

4
Strange Tales from Today

Scratches at the Door

When Cynthia moved into her new place in 1996, it was "pretty much a dream home." She had rented a cozy two-story townhouse condominium in a progressive housing co-op, nestled in a nook in Edmonton's river valley. She believed that she had found a sheltered refuge inside the bustle of the city, a close-knit community of friends and neighbors. As she unloaded the U-Haul, however, she did not suspect that she already had a roommate, a former occupant who would soon demand her attention.

When Cynthia first heard scratching sounds in the night, she tried to shrug them off as the kind of creaks and rattles every building makes—they take a while to get used to but eventually fade into the comfortable background. She held this opinion, she says, for about two seconds.

"I'm very psychically sensitive," explains Cynthia, who has experience in spirit communication and shamanism. "I knew pretty much instantly that this wasn't 'water pipes' or 'the house settling.' This was a message or impression from the other side." Soon, the scratching was accompanied by what Cynthia describes as a "psychic whine" and a feeling of loneliness and abandonment. Clearly, something was trapped in her new home and needed her help.

Through either intuition or psychic guidance, she focused her impromptu investigation on the basement. She found a sheet-metal plate screwed into the back of the basement door, covering its lower half. She removed the screws and lifted off the metal sheet.

"I wasn't surprised at what I found," she says. "The door was covered with deep scratches and gouges—claw marks. Obviously, a large dog had frantically pawed that door over a long period of time." A lifelong pet lover with a deep connection to the world of animals, Cynthia felt heartbroken by her discovery.

She began to ask neighbors about the townhouse's previous occupants, specifically about their pets. She soon found out that the earlier tenants, a busy professional couple with an active social life, had had a large white dog, perhaps a Samoyed. They kept it locked in the basement while they were at work during they day and while they were out at night—which was more often than not.

"They were totally irresponsible with that dog," says Cynthia. "They barely ever walked him, they were hardly ever home. That poor dog was pretty much just another piece of furniture, an ornament or status symbol of whatever." The neighbors, she says, often heard the dog whining and barking for hours in the basement. They didn't know what eventually became of the dog, but they stopped hearing or seeing it a few months before the couple moved away.

Cynthia continued to hear the scratching. Then, one day as she worked in her upstairs study, she caught a sudden glimpse of a large white dog. "I'm not usually very jumpy," she says, "but this made me drop my coffee cup." She realized the situation wouldn't resolve itself. She would have to deal directly with the lonely ghost dog.

"I decided to use my preferred method of communicating with spirits: plain, direct, honest, unafraid speech. I just spoke out loud to him. I said, 'You're welcome to stay here, but you are not allowed to frighten me or scare other people.' "

Again acting on intuition, she took a more concrete step. Leaving the broken mug and spilled coffee to be cleaned up later, she went straight downstairs, took the scarred basement door off its hinges and carried it out to the backyard.

"That weekend, I chopped the door to kindling and burned it. Some friends and I said a few prayers of peace over the fire." That was almost seven years ago, and since then Cynthia has never again heard the scratching or sensed the feeling of uncomprehending abandonment.

"I don't know whether it was my little speech or the symbolic removal of the door," says Cynthia, "but I like to believe that I gave that poor dog its freedom."

White Guardian Dogs

Few things are more terrifying than an aggressive dog. The sight of an otherwise innocent-looking animal suddenly possessed, with hackles raised and teeth bared, can inspire dread in even the most hardened postman. But as the following accounts show, some dogs must be cruel to be kind. These unlikely heroes, who materialize out of nowhere, share an inexplicable inclination to guide humans out of potentially fatal circumstances. For the bewildered few who encounter them, the experience is very much like being visited by a guardian angel.

A sudden California earthquake was still rumbling through Rita Swift's house as she stared in shock at the heavy brass lamp that had fallen across her pillow in a hail of shattered glass. A few short seconds earlier she had been lying in that exact spot. She would have been seriously injured or even killed had she not been frightened into motion by the sudden appearance of a fearsome canine apparition.

"I awoke to the clock radio playing louder than usual," Rita recalls in her account of the experience, which originally appeared in the January 2001 newsletter of the International Ghost Hunters' Society. "I asked my husband, Bill, to turn the music down, because I didn't want to wake our six-year-old daughter sleeping in the next room. I rolled over on my back, letting my right hand dangle loosely at the right side of the bed. I looked up at the hanging chain light centered above our bed, and saw it start to swing back and forth very slightly. Suddenly, I felt warm moist breath and something licking my right hand."

Rita turned to find herself staring into the piercing blue eyes of a 100-pound white Mastiff. "I can still visualize the bright pink loose skin around the dog's eyes," she writes, "and the foaming, smelly spit dripping from its dangling tongue. I watched it swallow, and I can remember how the muscles in its neck bulged. My hand felt hot and sticky."

Rita screamed and threw herself over her sleeping husband. She landed on the floor on the other side of their king-sized bed, dragging all of the bedclothes with her. Bill, jolted awake, grabbed his terrified wife in an instinctive protective embrace. An instant later, the confused and panicked couple felt the first sharp tremors of a major quake.

The scene erupted into pandemonium. "I remember screaming about the white dog. Our daughter, frightened of the earthquake, ran to our room and jumped on our bed. I searched the room with my eyes, trying to find the white dog that vanished. During the earthquake, a tall heavy walnut and brass lamp on my nightstand crashed over onto my pillow. The light bulb shattered on the headboard, spraying glass on my pillow, and the shade bounced across the bed. If my head had still been on my pillow, I could have been killed."

Rita is convinced that dog appeared—or was sent—to save her from imminent harm. "I do not scare easily," she says, "so if the white dog was my guardian angel, it had to go to extremes to get me out of harm's way. That was 30 years ago, but I can still see, feel and smell that white dog as if it were only yesterday."

Thirty years later, in the summer of 2000, the mysterious guardian reentered Rita's life. "I was reading and relaxing at our public library," she writes, "when my eyes focused on a magazine on a rack. A huge white Mastiff stared from the cover. An elderly lady sitting to my right was gazing at the cover. Our eyes met, and we started talking about the dog. I told her my story, and to my amazement, she answered with her own story of a strange white dog that once saved her life."

In 1942, 20-year-old Edna lived in Dearborn, Michigan. Like many young women during the war, she volunteered at a USO Canteen catering to servicemen. One night in mid-December, the place was particularly raucous—filled to bursting with music and laughter and thick clouds of cigarette smoke. After six hours in this atmosphere, Edna quite understandably developed a serious headache.

Closing time was less than half an hour away, so Edna asked a girlfriend to step outside with her for a breath of head-clearing fresh air before they got started on the night's cleanup. After a few minutes, Edna's friend went back into the canteen. Edna tried to follow, but as she approached the door a huge white dog came out of the mist and darkness, blocking her path.

Edna and the dog—"with eyes that were so evil"— faced each other. The slush-covered street was silent except for the muffled sounds of music and laughter from the canteen. Growling, the dog began to advance upon Edna, slowly forcing her down the street. Whenever she slowed down or stopped, the huge white dog bared its teeth and growled more menacingly.

Edna could feel the dog's barrel-like ribcage pushing against her legs as it herded her through the deserted winter streets and alleys. Wartime rationing prevented her from wearing stockings, but she could feel the dog's drool running down her legs onto her shoes. Too terrified to run or scream, Edna obeyed the white dog's snarls and nudges as it led her farther and farther from the warmth and safety of the servicemen's canteen.

Suddenly, in a moment of clarity through her terror, Edna realized that the white dog was leading her straight back to her home. The menacing creature knew the most direct route, pushing her through shortcuts and side streets she would never have walked alone at that time of night. When they reached her house, she climbed the front steps, the old wooden planks creaking in the night. She knew her parents were at home, asleep, but for some reason she didn't raise a cry of alarm or pound on the door for help. She just reached under the mat for the key, the white dog impatiently pushing and growling all the while, and entered the house.

Locking the door behind her, Edna looked back out through the door's small window. The huge dog still sat on the porch, staring back at her "as if it knew my every move." Edna found some soup bones on the kitchen counter and tossed them to the dog, opening the front door just wide enough to get her hand through. The motionless creature completely ignored the succulent offering. Suddenly, before Edna had turned away from the door, the hall telephone rang, piercing the silence of the sleeping house.

Unexpected telephone calls in the dead of night rarely bear happy news. Edna reached for the receiver with a sense of dread. A distraught co-worker from the canteen was at the other end of the line. Edna's girlfriend, with whom she had stepped out for air, had been shot and killed. Shortly after Edna had left, two drunken G.I.s began fighting over a woman. They drew their guns, and Edna's friend was caught in the back by a stray bullet. She had been cleaning up—the job Edna herself was supposed to have been doing.

Her mind reeling in shock and grief, Edna dropped the handset back into its cradle. In a daze, she noticed that the front door was still ajar. She walked over, opened the door and looked out on the porch. The white Mastiff was nowhere in sight, and the steakbones remained, untouched, on the doormat.

Later, at her friend's funeral, Edna was devastated and ashamed—classic symptoms of "survivor's guilt." If only I had stayed and finished my work, she thought, my friend would still be alive. She had cheated death, and her friend had paid the price.

Tormented, unable to concentrate on her studies or cope with her volunteer work, Edna returned to the cemetery a few days later to pray alone and beg forgiveness. In the fading light of a gray winter afternoon, she walked through a layer of freshly fallen snow to the mausoleum. She stayed there quietly

As she left the mausoleum, she looked across the now-dark cemetery and saw a private crypt draped with

A white Mastiff's threatening gestures ultimately saved a bewildered woman from certain death.

Christmas lights. She wondered idly how someone had managed to run electricity all the way out there. Suddenly she spotted the unmistakable form of the white dog, sitting on the steps of the crypt. Her heart in her throat, she locked eyes with the eerie animal. It glared steadily back at her with those same terrifying eyes. After a few seconds that felt like hours, it disappeared down the steps into the crypt.

Gathering her courage, Edna approached the oddly festive crypt. Under the bright Christmas lights, she looked for the dog's footprints in the fresh snow—and found none. The dog had disappeared without a trace, never to return.

"She told me that story, sitting across from me in the library," Rita says. "She tried to tell the story in the past, she said, but people usually assumed she wasn't playing with a full deck."

Of course, Rita knew better, in light of her own lifesaving encounter with the white Mastiff. And when she published her story in the Ghost Hunters' Society newsletter, she received letters from others with similar experiences. One such story takes place in Canton, Ohio, in 1955.

Nineteen-year-old Gracie should have been on top of the world. A pretty, energetic firefighter's daughter, she a had solid family, excellent friends and a good job in a lawyer's office. Unfortunately, like so many young women throughout history and literature, she chose the wrong man.

At first, he had seemed like an ideal catch—a handsome, athletic salesman, well on his way to becoming a rich man. Soon, though, Gracie realized that this "catch" came with a catch of his own: a viciously jealous, controlling ego.

After their first couple of dates, he began to treat Gracie like property. He kept tabs on her every move, demanding to know who she talked to and what they talked about, and flew into rages whenever he decided in his paranoia that she'd been "making time" with other men.

Gracie tried to break things off, but he wouldn't be denied. He followed her around the neigborhood in his car, made threatening phone calls and spread savage rumors. Gracie's father eventually confronted him, threatening to have him arrested if the stalking continued.

For a while, the threat seemed to have worked. Then, one Sunday afternoon, Gracie was in her front yard picking flowers when she saw his car pulling over to the curb. She dropped the flowers and ran for the front door.

Before she had taken two strides, an enormous white bulldog burst from the hedges. Snarling, it blocked her path to the door and chased her around the side of the house. She lost her footing and stumbled down the cellar steps, falling in through the open door. Her father and brother, who were working on the furnace, looked up in time to see the huge white dog following her down the steps. Suddenly, the air was shattered by the sound of multiple rifle shots from the front yard.

The stalker, filled with lethal jealousy, assumed Gracie had gone in through the front door. He fired round after round through the windows and walls. When only one bullet remained, he turned the gun on himself.

Gracie and her family never saw the snarling white dog again. But they remain certain that it had deliberately saved her life that afternoon, by driving her away from the front of the house.

Over the years, Rita has tried without success to determine the breed of the mysterious guardian dog. "I own two AKC American and International Champion Italian Greyhounds," she says, "and at all the shows I have attended throughout the years, I have never seen a dog like it. I have even bought books about rare and extinct dogs, but again with no luck. That white dog was one of a kind."

On that coincidental afternoon in the library, Rita and Edna agreed that the dog had changed their image of the stereotypical guardian angel. "Edna was raised Catholic," Rita says, "and always believed guardian angels were beautiful, with feathered white wings. To be honest, I believed the same story.

"Now, I think we were both wrong. If a life must be saved, our angels have to go to desperate extremes."

Uncle Hart's
Cat-haunted Chair

Outdoorsman, prospector, logger and surveyor. Story-teller, soldier and two-fisted hell in a fight. Hart Christie was one of those larger-than-life characters who define the Western spirit. But Hart Christie was also a prankster and top-notch teller of tall tales. The tallest of these haunts his descendants to this day.

Born an Alberta farm boy just before the turn of the century, the restless young Hart soon decided he wanted more out of life than farming could offer. By age 13, he had already run off to Edmonton twice. Three years later he was gone for good, to the wilderness of British Columbia's interior.

Nobody knows for sure what Hart had planned when he packed his bags—a job in the logging camps, maybe, or the instant riches of a gold find, or both, or neither? Uncle Hart told dozens of tales, tall and otherwise, all of them worth retelling. There was the time a drunken logger woke up hungover and 20 feet up a tree, with Hart and the rest of the crew laughing below. Or the time Hart fashioned a hidden, eerie-sounding set of wind chimes out of his cooking gear, to guard his camp in a reportedly "haunted" area.

Stories aside, we know a few things for certain about those days. By 1912, Hart had found a place on a sur-veying crew, helping to build the Grand Trunk Pacific Railway. By 1915, he was in Europe, fighting in the

The eerie spirit of a cat haunts a chair owned by a descendant of the adventurer Hart Christie.

First World War. His experiences there would probably fill two books, but in the end he was one of the lucky ones who made it back alive. Like many war veterans, he found that the horrors of combat quenched his thirst for adventure. He returned home to the life he'd fled as a teenager—working his land, raising his family and telling his stories.

That's not to say that Hart Christie became what you'd call a conventional man. Where he once threw his restless energy into wandering western Canada in search of fortune, he now threw it into collecting weird artifacts. His house brimmed with a motley collection of stuffed and mounted animals, fossils, old weapons and strange pieces of old furniture. Of course, every item had a story, but one of them had a doozy. A bizarrely carved straight-backed chair, according to family legend, was home to a malevolent feline ghost.

That chair, or at least the last surviving part of it, now rests in the hands of Hart's great-great nephew and namesake, the younger Hart Christie. He uncovered the chair's back piece while cleaning out his grandmother's overstuffed basement.

"The junk down there was packed 20 feet deep," he recalls. "Some of it probably hadn't been seen, let alone moved, in 40 years or more. I worked away at the pile all day, and eventually I pulled this weird old wood carving out from a spot way at the back." A leering gargoyle, its tongue stuck out, gazed out from the red-stained slab of dark hardwood. Deeply carved designs surrounded the taunting face, covering every inch of the board. "I didn't know what it was, or if it was valuable, so I brought it up and asked Grandma about it.

"As soon as she saw it, her eyes went wide. She said, 'Oh my God! I can't believe I've had that in my house all this time and didn't know it.' I asked her what she meant, and she told me this crazy story about the 'Cat Chair' that Uncle Hart had brought back from Europe."

Seems nobody knows whether the story began with Uncle Hart, or if his adoring (and ghost-story-loving) nephews and nieces concocted it later. Uncle Hart may have picked up on one of the older cousins' own crude spook stories, embroidered it and repeated it back to children who'd forgotten—or chose not to remember—that they'd invented the story in the first place. Either way, the Cat Chair became a mysterious and powerful object of legend among the Christie clan's younger generation.

The chair's precise origins remain murky. Did it come from Italy, Spain, France or elsewhere? Perhaps it had been smuggled out of Russia by a rich czarist family fleeing Bolshevik persecution. It may have been purchased normally, won in a card game or—the most popular theory—looted from a ruined mansion, the only piece of wood that hadn't been reduced to ashes and kindling by shelling and fire.

Apparently, though, it had once been the property of a European witch. She sat on that very chair while casting spells of luck, love and revenge for the Italian (or Spanish or French or Russian) townsfolk. The chair never stood empty; whenever the witch got up from the chair, her black cat took her place.

When the old woman died—or was killed or mysteriously vanished—her faithful cat planted itself firmly on the chair's deep-red leather seat. Refusing any food and water, the cat soon followed its mistress to the grave.

When Uncle Hart brought the chair home, his wife, Ellen, adamantly refused to allow "that hideous thing" anywhere guests might see it. Eventually it ended up in Hart's study, a tiny room at the back of the house. Aunt Ellen's objections may have gone deeper than mere personal taste. Ellen reputedly had a bit of "second sight," and the Cat Chair gave her a serious case of the creeps. For her own peace of mind, she relegated it to the farthest corner of the house.

The tactic must have failed, considering the feline spirit's subsequent mischief.

The Christies had no flesh-and-blood housecats, but the ghost cat more than made up for that. It took care of the responsibilities of your average pet kitty, knocking things over and keeping people awake at night. If Aunt Ellen complained that her china cabinet had been disturbed, Hart would blame the cat. Scratching sounds or strange creaks in the night? "There goes that cat again." Eventually, the invisible cat became an all-purpose gremlin, blamed for every petty household nuisance.

Uncle Hart wasn't the only one who believed in the cat. The Christies kept several barn cats around the farm to keep the mice down, and they refused to ever set a paw inside the house. Hart and his young relatives contended that the ghost cat chased them away.

"My Grandma said that her Uncle Hart simply liked to yank the kids' chains," says the younger Hart. "He built up the goofy ghost story until she and the other kids actually believed it. Even as she told me the story, she seemed genuinely amazed that She had this piece of the old chair in her house without having the ghost cat that came with it."

Like his great-great-uncle, young Hart loved to collect strange, miscellaneous knickknacks. He offered to take the legendary hunk of wood home with him, and his grandmother readily agreed. She wanted it out of the house, even though it hadn't caused her any problems during decades of storage.

"It's kind of cool-looking," says Hart, "and I love having family items, especially when they have good stories attached to them. I may even start the legend up again when my nieces get older."

When Hart took the back of the chair home, however, he began to wonder whether the family legend contained a grain of truth. "I propped the chair up in this corner of my computer room. My cat Spock came into the room to say hello and check out what I'd bought.

"As soon as Spock saw the chair back, he jumped about three feet straight up. When he landed, he stood on his hind legs and yowled. Seriously—he stood there with his paws out like a begging dog, making this incredibly freaky wailing sound. It was like he was praying to some kind of pagan Cat God or something. After about five seconds, he bolted out of the room as fast as I've ever seen him run.

"It's the weirdest thing I've ever seen a cat do—and I've seen cats do plenty of weird things."

Spock never came back into the room, as long as Hart kept the spooky old scrap of furniture. "He used to sit on top of the monitor for the heat when I was working," Hart explains, "but after I'd brought in the gargoyle carving he'd just sit out in the hallway and meow. That got annoying really quick, so I moved the chair back into the bedroom. I figured at last I had found a way to keep him from spraying on the bed."

The chair didn't stay in the bedroom for long either. "It kept Spock out," Hart explains, "but my fiancée told me to get rid of it because it gave her the creeps."

Finally, the creepy old carving found a home out in the garage. "That's the last refuge for all the things my fiancée doesn't want in the house," Hart laughs.

"I'm not saying that I believe the chair really is possessed by a spirit," Hart adds, "and I definitely doubt that stuff about the 'European witch.' It's probably just an ugly, spooky old thing that scares women, children and small animals.

"But when you see a cat freak out like that, you can't help but wonder."

The Moose That Wasn't There

Renowned psychic, healer and Reiki master Kay Mora of St. Augustine, Florida, built up a lifetime of accomplishments before passing away in February 2003 at the age of 74. The founder of the Metaphysical Mother Earth Church, she appeared regularly on television and radio programs around the world. In her role as a professional psychic, also known as Kaimora, she assisted police in several states, as well as the FBI and the International Crime Commission of the Virgin Islands.

Those who knew her best, however, remember Kaimora as a beloved teacher. Her workshops, lectures, radio programs and learning centers helped many people realize their potential through holistic thinking.

She also provided a wellspring of stories and anecdotes. Brian Dean, a Reiki practitioner in Jacksonville, Florida, relates Kaimora's tale of a unique phantom animal—an apparition apparently created through the power of the human mind.

In 1996, Kaimora attended a small concert near her summer home in Maine. Afterward, she struck up a conversation with the musicians, a quartet from New York, and found they had a few days free. She invited them to spend the time at her place, promising them a very calming and spiritual time.

The following afternoon, the group sat discussing the area's wildlife, especially the famous moose that roam Maine's forests. The New Yorkers said they'd never seen one of these majestic creatures. Kay said that a pair of moose regularly watched television through her neighbors' windows, but they hadn't appeared that evening. Kay offered to drive the musicians up a nearby mountain to enjoy the sunset and perhaps spot a moose or two.

The sunset indeed proved beautiful, but the group still felt disappointed. All the way up and half the way back, and they still hadn't seen a moose. Not wanting to disappoint her guests, Kay went for Plan B. Slowing the car and rolling down her window, she tried out her best moose call. First in a mid-range pitch, and then lower, she sent her eerie mooing sounds into the trees. After a few minutes, a huge bull moose with an amazing eight-foot rack of antlers glided out of the forest.

Everyone got out of the car and began taking pictures in the twilight. The huge moose, rummaging placidly in the roadside grass, didn't seem to mind the bright flashes. The enchanted New Yorkers asked Kay if it would be all right to walk up to the moose and touch it. Kay wisely explained that the woods aren't petting zoos. Get too close to a bull moose, she said, and he'll quickly show you what those enormous antlers are for.

By this time, at least 20 other cars had stopped for the moose. Strangely, the animal didn't seem annoyed or frightened by all the noise and attention. It simply stood there in the long grass, chewing its cud. Since the moose didn't seem inclined to wander away, the musicians decided to take some posed pictures. First they stood in front of the moose, then Kay and so on. When their film ran out, they bid farewell to the patient moose and drove on.

A few months later, Kay traveled to New York to visit her new friends. As they sat around and visited, the

*A moose that Kay and her friends had photographed disappeared
inexplicably from the developed prints.*

conversation drifted back to the day they saw the moose.
Kay's hosts exchanged significant glances and asked her if
she'd like to see the photos. The four of them each
brought out their own set of photos from the weekend—
Kay's house, the drive up the mountain, the sunset and
finally the wooded roadside where they stopped to see
the moose.

As she flipped through the photos, Kay's jaw dropped lower and lower. She saw the trees, the cars, and the people in various poses but—no moose. Each photo was clean and in focus, with an empty space where the moose should have been. None of the pictures contained the slightest glimpse of the animal.

Despite her surprise, Kay was not as shocked as her hosts expected. She explained that strong conscious or subconscious desires can sometimes create seemingly real objects. Some Tibetan lamas, for example, are said to use their imagination and concentration to create tulpas—entities that appear physically real and may even seem to display independent will.

Kay believed that this explained the events in the Maine woods. Her friends' unified longing to see a moose, combined with the psychic's trained mind, conjured a magnificent moose into a roadside reality.

Amazingly, Kay had another similar experience about a month later. Two of her students, a male bank president and a female technician, had been making little progress in her class. Locked into a skeptical worldview, they couldn't open up to spiritual experiences. Kay suggested that a trip into the Maine wilderness might help.

At the cabin, Kay told the story of her earlier guests and their moose. Her two students had a bit of a laugh. The musicians had simply flubbed their snapshots, they said, either by pressing the shutter after the moose had moved off, or by simply framing them poorly in the first place. They assured Kay that, unlike the musicians, they knew how to use their cameras. They wouldn't make the same mistake.

So, piling their photo gear into her car, Kay took her guests up the mountain to see the sunset. As before, nobody spotted a moose on the drive up. On the way back, Kay once again slowed the car and did her moose call. This time, she managed to attract moose more than once. The two delighted shutterbugs shot several rolls of the various moose, experimenting with different lenses and shutter speeds. They returned to Kay's house happy and satisfied.

Soon after the visit, though, the woman telephoned Kay. Her voice shook as she described what she and the bank president found when they opened their packets of prints: photo after photo of trees and grass, roadside and ditch, but not a single moose. Not one. There was nothing wrong with their cameras, no fault in the film. Every shot was perfectly composed, missing only the moose. They could find no rational explanation for what they saw in the photos—or, rather, didn't see.

It had been a shattering experience, the woman told Kay, an overwhelming revelation for both of them. The bank president had resigned his hard-won and lucrative position, sold off his material possessions and headed "out west" to live. She had similar plans: to head to Nevada and meditate in peace and quiet, to adjust her mind to her new and radically altered perspective. Kay never heard from either of them again.

The Whoosh Cat

One beautiful late-summer day in the countryside outside Memphis, Tennessee, Jeff was relaxing in the sun on his backyard patio, grilling up some steaks on the barbecue and enjoying a cold beer. Everything seemed perfect, until out of nowhere he felt an insistent tugging at the back of his mind, some outside force that compelled him away from his beef and beer.

"I felt a strange, overwhelming compulsion to get up and go look into the front yard," says Jeff. As he walked around the house, he began to hear an eerie noise, growing gradually louder. "It was a strange rushing sound," he says, "like a strong wind, only there was no wind."

By the time he reached the front corner of the house, the whooshing sound had become a head-splitting white noise. It seemed to come from everywhere, surrounding him. He looked around the corner and saw a huge cat in the front yard. "It was about three feet tall at the shoulder, with very long legs," he says. As the roaring howl reached deafening proportions, the cat bounded across the drive and raced away at an amazing speed, disappearing over the top of the hill bordering Jeff's property.

The rushing sound promptly faded, leaving a profound silence in the hot Tennessee air. But the strange, insistent compulsion that gripped Jeff's mind didn't fade so quickly. "I felt I just had to chase after it," says Jeff.

Within seconds, Jeff had sprinted up the hill. From the top, he looked out across the expansive landscape. He couldn't see the cat anywhere. Even at the speed the cat had been running, it couldn't have topped another hill and gone out of sight in such a short time. It had just vanished.

As Jeff stood there, a feeling of irrational dread crept over him. "I suddenly felt wary," he says, "like something was watching me or waiting for me." The feeling passed, but left a vague uneasiness, a sense of unseen, malicious forces at work. Disturbed, he turned around and went back to the house.

"I told my wife," he says, "and her response was tepid." She chalked it up as just another in a series of weird but harmless phenomena the couple had experienced at the house. "We'd hear people talking and moving around in unoccupied rooms, or we'd catch movement and figures out of the corners of our eyes," says Jeff. "My wife's a confirmed skeptic, but four years in that house convinced her that there was something there."

Over time, Jeff had identified four distinct ghosts in the house. The first was his maternal grandmother, a mean-spirited old woman who originally owned the place. The second, his paternal grandfather, died in an upper room of the house. The third, a man named Arthur Dumas, had been smitten by Jeff's grandmother. When she refused to marry him, he stalked her until he was arrested and locked up in an insane asylum, where he eventually died. Jeff and his wife could not determine the identity of the fourth ghost, a little girl.

The paranormal activity seemed particularly concentrated in one hallway. In addition to the usual weird voices and disturbing half-glimpses of motion, guests often described a feeling of dread as they walked down the hallway. They felt as if they had entered a place where they were deeply unwelcome. "It was my grandmother," says Jeff. "Her spirit was particularly bad at times. She did not go gently into that good night. Everyone who ever visited us hated to go up there after dark, but that hall was the only way to the bathroom."

Jeff's grandfather limited himself to flickering on the edges of people's vision, but Arthur Dumas actually showed up in full visual form. Before Jeff's grandmother died, Dumas appeared twice: once to Jeff's mother, and once to a lady who shared the house with Jeff's grandmother. More recently, his ghost lurked unseen in the front yard, spying on the woman who spurned him. Says Jeff, "He seemed to hide behind this tree at the end of the driveway. Our dog always focused on that tree to the exclusion of all others, staring at it and growling."

Jeff says that the child "was the strangest of all because we don't know where she came from." They first became aware of her when Jeff's young niece came for a visit. She tugged on her uncle's shirtsleeve and said, with her eyes wide in amazement, "There's a girl living in your fireplace!" Another grown-up might have chalked this experience up to a child's overactive imagination, but Jeff had lived too long in the house to discount anything.

"After that," he says, "we heard this girl laugh on several occasions." Although it sounded like a happy girlish giggle, it carried an underlying aura of despair and malevolence. "Once she screamed in terror," Jeff continues, "and scared the hell out of all of us—including our cat, who spontaneously vomited."

Because Jeff's wife had grown accustomed to living in a house packed with ghosts, it's no wonder she was ready to shrug off the strange cat creature in the front yard. According to Jeff, though, the story of what he calls the "Whoosh Cat" didn't end with its disappearance over the hill.

"Our neighbor lived in a small house at the top of that hill," he explains. "The cat, had it not disappeared, would have crossed right through his front yard." Several weeks after Jeff saw the Whoosh Cat, the neighbor's house burned to the ground.

"The fire department arrived in time to save it," says Jeff, "but they had a hard time getting the water pumped up the hill. For some reason, it took three engines to get the water to the house. By then it was gone." In a vivid dream a few days later, a voice told Jeff that a spirit of fire inhabited the hill.

Slowly, Jeff made a connection. "The hill on the other side of us also has a house on it," he says, "or, rather, it had a house on it. About the time I saw the Whoosh Cat, that house was gutted by fire. First them, and now my other neighbor. If you draw between those two fires, it crosses my front yard right where the cat appeared.

"That did it for me. We moved. The whole time we lived in that house, I'd had a premonition of fire. I felt sure that if we stayed there any longer, it was going to get to us."

Neither Jeff nor his wife regret leaving the old place behind. Says Jeff, "It's nice to be able to get up in the middle of the night and walk around the house without feeling like there's someone behind you all the time. These were not harmless or friendly spirits."

Hounded!

Seventeen-year-old Gwen sat on the Greyhound bus, making the long trip south from her home in Oregon to her Aunt Joan's place in Arizona. Her mother hoped that Gwen's allergy-related asthma, which had become steadily worse through adolescence, would respond well to the arid climate. She also felt Gwen needed the broadening effect of travel.

"I can't send you to France, but I can send you to Phoenix," she joked. Gwen failed to see the humor. Her mother constantly worried that Gwen would end up "lost in books"—undersocialized, never realizing any dream outside their small city. With a teenager's cynicism, Gwen had a cruel but honest interpretation of her mother's concern: She just doesn't want me to end up like her.

But as the bus finally pulled into the terminal, she felt a surge of excitement. She'd never visited her Arizona relatives, though they'd been up to the Pacific Northwest. She looked forward to getting to know her cousin Peggy, who was just less than a year older than her. The two of them would be going to the same college. She was also anxious to see if the desert air would improve her breathing. She fantasized about the day when she could toss away her ever-present inhaler. Jittery but hopeful, she stepped off the bus and into the Arizona sunshine.

Aunt Joan's boyfriend, Roy, had come to pick her up. A nervous and insecure guy who tried to compensate by being overly manly, he gave Gwen bad vibes right away. "He didn't really smile at me. He just gave me one of those non-smile grimaces," Gwen recalls. "And I remember him shaking my hand way too hard, like we had just done some kind of business deal or something. I guess I overreacted, but I was a shy teenager. My dad died when I was five so I never really had a father figure around. Any kind of macho stuff sort of scared me."

Perhaps, Gwen thought, she was just feeling the stress of moving to an unfamiliar town. As they drove to her new home, she occupied her mind with the sights passing by the windows. Soon they pulled up to the house, a large flat-roofed bungalow with stucco walls and a rounded front living-room wall. Aunt Joan ran out to meet her.

"She was genuinely delighted to have me there," Gwen recalls, "and so was my cousin. It was like we were instantly sisters, all three of us. At that moment, whatever dark clouds I sensed just went away. I even imagined I was breathing better, although there's no way my asthma could have gotten better that quickly. I just felt good."

Little did they suspect, as they trucked Gwen's bags into the house, that the house was about to receive its first visit from the frightening entity they eventually knew as "the Dog."

"We didn't hear about it until way later, after a lot of the other stuff had happened," Gwen says. "But I guess Roy first encountered the Dog on the same night." Gwen says. "Aunt Joan told us about it eventually. Maybe Roy made it up, or convinced itself that it happened after things started to get crazy. I don't know."

According to Roy, he had slept on the couch in the living room that night because his snoring was keeping Joan awake. After a few hours of restless tossing and turning he

In a strange story from Arizona, a black dog drives an angry man to distraction but doesn't affect others in the same house.

felt chilly and realized that his blanket had fallen to the floor. He reached down and tried to tug it back onto the couch, but it seemed to snag on something. He rolled over and came face-to-face with a huge black dog, its fiery eyes glowing red in the darkened room.

"He called it a 'black dog,' but said it was actually kind of invisible," Gwen says. "He had the impression that he was looking at a dog, although the only things he really saw were its eyes." The dog glowered across the blanket at the scared-stiff Roy, exuding an aura of malevolence and menace, then faded away. Roy must have fallen asleep immediately—strange, after such a frightening experience—because the next thing he remembered was waking up the next morning.

Gwen didn't encounter the dog until after she had settled in and gotten to know the area with her cousin. Unlike Roy's night terrors, Gwen's contact seemed relatively benign. "About 10 days after I moved in, I started hearing a dog whimpering at night, maybe three times a week or so," she says. "I thought some neighbor's dog must not like being left outside." At first, the sound didn't particularly disturb her. Gwen would rouse slightly at the noise and then fall easily back to sleep. Soon, however, things began to intensify.

"After a while the whimper became more insistent, more of a full-on whine," she says. It sounded less like a dog begging to be let in and more like a threat. Gwen no longer found it easy to fall back to sleep.

One morning over coffee, about three weeks after she moved in, Gwen happened to mention the dog to her cousin. Peggy replied, "Has that dog been waking you up too?" She had no idea whose dog it could be. The cousins decided to ask around the neighborhood, but nobody else had heard any whining in the night, and nobody knew of any new dogs in the area.

Gwen and Peggy began to get creeped out. Something wasn't right. The more they thought about it, the more they believed that this wasn't just some dog or coyote making noise at night. In some ways, it didn't even seem like a real sound—once they woke up, everything was quiet. The girls tried to be "Little Miss Rational," as Gwen puts it. They came up with theories of water pipes and crickets and rusty gate hinges, but they felt otherwise.

By this point, the girls no longer felt comfortable alone in the dark. They started having "slumber parties," sleeping on the floor of each other's rooms. The nighttime whining grew less frequent, but when it did happen it sounded more menacing. It had turned into a growl.

Now, when the girls woke up to the sound, they were chilled by an unsettling new feeling. "It's not like we felt threatened," says Gwen. "It was more like the feeling you get when you're walking your dog and all of a sudden it starts growling for no reason. Apprehension, you know?"

While this continued at night, day-to-day life in the house took a turn for the worse. Roy's temper grew shorter and shorter, his moods became more unpredictable. His company had just laid off a large number of workers, and although Roy had kept his job, he was working harder than ever. He pulled double shifts and split shifts, with the specter of another round of layoffs hanging over him. He'd always had a stereotypical "Man of the House" attitude, but he had become downright domineering. He also began drinking heavily.

Aunt Joan couldn't hide the strain. Her cheerfulness had a desperate tone to it, and bags appeared under her eyes. She and Roy quarrelled almost daily, poisoning the atmosphere in the house. Gwen wanted more than any-thing to go home, even though she was starting college in a few short weeks. Finally, Peggy (who had never warmed up to her mother's new boyfriend) asked Joan point-blank: "What's wrong with Roy?"

"It all came out, then," says Gwen—Roy's nightmares, the visions of being watched by a menacing Dog in the night, the story of his first face-to-face with the Dog. For weeks now, Joan had also glimpsed a dark animal out of the corner of her eye, but it always vanished when she turned to look. She had shrugged it off as a stress reac-tion, a response to the layoffs, the uncertainty. But when she heard what Gwen and Peggy had been experiencing, her face went white.

"Mom," said Peggy, "I think someone's trying to tell us something. I think we're in danger."

Joan didn't say anything—she didn't need to. Supernatural forces or not, Roy had clearly gone off the rails. It was only a matter of time before he lashed out and hurt somebody. "Aunt Joan didn't know what to do," Gwen recalls. "She was as freaked out as we were. Peggy told me things had been pretty bad for a while, but now everything was about to explode."

Two days later, that's exactly what happened. Gwen and Penny returned from a shopping trip to hear Joan and Roy—mostly Roy—shouting from inside the house. The girls carried their bags up the front stairs and banged noisily through the door, hoping that their arrival would, as usual, cause Roy to break off his tirade and storm sul-lenly off.

Not this time. Roy stood in his bedclothes over Joan, who had backed herself into a corner of the couch. He whirled, red-faced, when the girls entered, and began cursing incoherently at Gwen.

"You can't print most of the things he yelled at me," she recalls. "He called me every name and four-letter word in the book. He said I'd corrupted Peggy, that I'd turned 'his woman' against him, that I was possessed, that I was a witch, that I should be killed, that I'd put a curse on him and a curse on 'his house'—which it wasn't, by the way.

"I felt paralyzed with shock. I remember just sinking to the floor and cowering, curled up and crying. I thought he was going to hit me, maybe kill me. It was the most frightening moment of my life."

Joan could take it no longer. With steel in her voice, she told Peggy to call the cops. That got Roy's attention. He turned, amazed, to see Joan standing tall. "Get out," she said. "Get out now, get out fast and don't come back." Roy stood there for a moment, nearly purple with rage, before thundering out of the house and roaring away in his truck.

Later, when Gwen had calmed down and rested, the girls learned what had happened while they were out. Roy had worked the graveyard shift the previous night and was sleeping while Joan did some work in the yard. Around two o'clock in the afternoon, Joan heard him screaming. She ran into the house and found him on the floor outside their bedroom, trembling with a chaotic mix of rage and terror.

He had seen the Dog again, he said, the black something that had terrorized him for nearly two months. It wasn't a dream this time, he said, it couldn't be a dream. The Dog had clamped its jaws on his shoulder and dragged him out of bed, shaking its head to solidly set its teeth, like a dog playing tug-of-war. That cursed dog would get him eventually, he said, and it was all Gwen's fault.

Had Roy been driven mad by a malicious spirit? Did Gwen's own fear and anxiety create a monster? Or was the Dog a protective entity, acting to remove a threat to the family? Gwen, who still lives in Arizona and breathes much easier, chooses not to speculate. Neither she nor Peggy ever felt directly threatened by the Dog, she says.

"I was scared stiff, but not of the Dog. I felt like it was trying to fight off an approaching threat, or warn me about it." Once Roy had left the house—an embarrassed mutual friend packed up his stuff later that week—the Dog never returned.

The Thing in the Middle of Nowhere

Norman stood in the front room of the cabin, shaking with rage and terror. His white knuckles gripped the rifle, a cheap little .22 he'd had since he was a kid—a farm boy's first firearm. He probably hadn't set the sights since he was a teenager, 20 years ago. He laughed inwardly, morbidly, at this train of thought. As if the sights mattered. Even if his aim were dead-on, there's nothing his pathetic popgun—or any gun—could do to the thing lurking outside. But at least the gun was something, a symbol of defiance against the creature that was prowling his property, stalking him, stalking his wife.

Stalking his wife!

The only illumination came from the moonlight filtering in through the big windowed front wall of the old A-frame. Norman didn't really know this cabin. He and Michelle hadn't spent enough time in it to make it familiar, to make it really theirs. But they had liked it from the moment the sales agent had first shown them the photos. Decorated in the late '70s, the place reflected that decade's rustic ideals, from the rough country-style furniture to the big cedar hot tub—a bit of Colorado by way of Northern California. "Rocky Mountain High," Michelle had joked. She was a diehard John Denver fan from way back, and for her the cabin was a teenage fantasy come to life.

Well, it wasn't exactly the Rockies, but it was close. Built on the shores of a mountain lake a few hours north of Kamloops, British Columbia, the cabin couldn't be beat for "getting away from it all." The property was inaccessible by road—vacationers had to take a motorboat or hike down through the forest along a nearly nonexistent trail. It had no phone or electricity, but it had a propane refrigerator and lighting system. Running water came courtesy of a water-box in the creek above the cabin, filtered for drinking. The nearest neighbor was three undeveloped five-acre lots away through the trees. Eagles nested nearby, flying squirrels came out at sunset and kokanee salmon ran in the lake.

Norman and Michelle had pictured the cabin as a happy, homey place to spend long summer weekends with family and friends—and, they hoped, children. It was their dream home.

Dream home? More like a nightmare now, thought Norman.

Not long after they spent their first exhausting but happy four-day weekend there, the trouble began. First came an unexpected and bitter power struggle in Norman's workplace. Because of his position, he was unavoidably drawn into the battle. He had survived, probably ending up more secure than ever, but the effort had left him physically and mentally exhausted—totally unprepared for what came next.

Michelle had fallen from a stepladder while hanging curtains. She hadn't injured herself too badly—a mild concussion, a sprained wrist, bruises—but the damage went deeper. She and Norman had been trying for years to start a family, and just a week earlier she had found out she was pregnant. Shortly after her accident, she lost the baby. They couldn't tell whether her fall had caused the miscarriage, but she couldn't help feeling that it had been her fault.

Norman and Michelle felt emotionally depleted. They knew they had to retreat and recharge. They arranged for time off from work and headed out to the cabin on the lake. As the pickup's wheels ate up the miles of highway, they felt their mood lighten. Singing along to their old country and western tapes, they rolled hopefully towards their future.

Their upbeat mood didn't last. As Norman steered their overloaded motorboat around the point and the cabin first came into view, he felt a sudden sinking feeling, a surge of despair. The trim little A-frame seemed hostile rather than welcoming. He sensed a threat lurking in the hidden depths of the otherwise beautiful woods. He gave his head a shake, blaming the feelings on his own mental exhaustion. But that flash of fear proved just the beginning.

The next two days were miserable. Norman and his wife spent much of the time bickering irritably over little nothings. All the while they continued to feel that sense of menace, of being watched, as if something just out of sight was looking on and laughing. On occasions they both heard their names called as they worked, but when they turned their heads their spouse was nowhere to be seen. They chalked it up to nerves and unfamiliar surroundings—anything but the idea that there was actually something out there, stalking them.

The nights were even worse. They thrashed in their sleep, tormented by dark dreams of being watched, hunted. Inhuman yellow eyes, cat's eyes, stared out of impossibly dense thickets, radiating menace and mockery. They woke drenched in sweat, panicking in the cabin's dark sleeping loft, certain they'd heard something outside the cabin. Waves of malice from the forest seemed to break over the walls of the cabin.

On the third day, the negative emotions reached an intolerable level. Norman and Michelle both felt like they could scream or cry at any moment, but neither felt able to tell the other what they were feeling. They felt ashamed, worthless and could barely speak to each other without snapping angrily. They spent the day apart, trying to lose themselves in repetitive physical work. Norman washed windows and sanded the deck, while Michelle tended to the neglected flower beds leading from the waterfront to the cabin. At about two o'clock in the hot afternoon, Michelle decided to cool off with a swim.

Diving through the upper layer of sun-warmed water into the colder depths below, she let the icy chill of the lake electrify her body and scour away the murky mental haze. Surfacing again into the bright sunshine, floating on her back on the crystal waters, she began to feel happy and peaceful once more, for the first time in days. They were just tired, she told herself, tired and hurt. All they needed was time, sunshine and the clear mountain lake. Everything would be okay.

That's when it hit her again, the overwhelming sense of mocking hostility, of despair and hopelessness. The cold water no longer felt refreshing; its icy fingers reached into her body, numbing her, dragging her down. From the trees at the shoreline, she knew something was watching her, something unmistakably feline. She felt it stare at her, amused and inhuman. Then, just as suddenly, it was gone.

In a rush of panic, she thrashed desperately toward the beach. It seemed a million miles away, but she somehow made it. She hauled herself sputtering onto the sand and lay panting against a big fallen log. Norman called down from the cabin, asking if she was all right. "I'm fine," she called back. For a long time she huddled there, out of sight of the cabin, composing herself. She couldn't let Norman see her like this. He wouldn't understand.

That evening, a massive thunderstorm rolled over the valley, churning up whitecaps on the lake and pelting the cabin with sheet after sheet of driving rain. The weather outside seemed to reflect the storm brewing inside the little A-frame. The couple teetered on the verge of breakdown, terrified by their inexplicable emotions and by the cat thing that watched them. They could barely stand being near one another but there was no way to get distance in the cabin. They had a fireplace and brandy, and with a storm outside they should have felt cozy. Instead, the cabin seemed intolerably cramped, like a submarine. They gulped their brandy rather than sipping it and brooded miserably by the fire, unable to enjoy its warmth. Outside, they both knew, their unnatural stalker waited and watched in evil satisfaction.

Finally the haunted couple, hollow-eyed and exhausted, simply collapsed into chairs on opposite sides of the room. They stared at books and magazines without really reading anything, waiting for the clock to roll around to a reasonable hour for bedtime. At around nine o'clock, with the storm still raging over the lake, they drank a final few fingers of brandy and headed up to bed, hoping for sleep. Fatigue, it turns out, can be stronger than fear; they were asleep before their heads hit their pillows.

After a few hours of deep, dreamless sleep, the couple awoke simultaneously, coming up wide-eyed and frantic. They felt as if no time had passed, but the thunderstorm was gone, leaving only the wind-rustling of the trees in the midnight forest. They stared at each other fearfully, their faces illuminated in the moonlight. They knew they had awoken suddenly because something wanted them awake—awake to be terrorized. They lay breathing raggedly, unable to move, as the sounds began outside.

It began with the snap of twigs and the crunch of undergrowth, as something large circled the cabin. They didn't have to strain to hear it; whatever it was, it wasn't concerned about moving quietly. They heard the rasp of animal breathing, huge gusts of air heaved in and out of a deep chest—half the sound of an animal tracking a scent, half the sound of hoarsely whispered laughter: hunff-hunf-hunnff-hunnhh. Malice and terror filled the damp forest air.

For 15 minutes—or 15 lifetimes—the thing paced around the cabin, its hide scraping against the rough walls. Hatred flowed in from outside, lodging itself with cold heat in the hearts of the petrified couple. For the first time, they felt horribly aware of their isolation, here in the middle of nowhere. Michelle stared wide-eyed at her husband, trembling more and more violently. She struggled to keep from screaming, teeth clenched, breathing harsh and fast through her nose, hot tears pouring from the corners of her eyes.

Finally, she broke loose. With a cry somewhere between a terrified scream and a despondent howl, she threw her arms around Norman's neck. She buried her face in his chest, clinging to him, wailing uncontrollably with the force of days, weeks, of unstopped emotion. And with every one of her screams and sobs there came an answering cry from the thing outside, a savage and shrill cat yowl, a soul-piercing parody of human misery and despair.

With every one of Michelle's screaming sobs, with every one of the unseen creature's sadistic, mocking responses, a piece of Norman's cold fear changed into a burning ember of rage. Eventually, he built up enough anger to propel him into motion. When his wife loosened her grip on his neck and collapsed onto the bedspread, Norman swung out of bed and grabbed his rifle.

Now, standing in the cabin's front room, he looked down at his weapon. In his adult hands his boyhood treasure looked almost silly, a toylike thing of cheap steel and cheaper wood. Once, this pathetic little gun had made him feel like a Big Man, grown-up, responsible, ready. But now?

The waves of heat radiating from outside had beaten him down, destroying his fragile courage. His rifle was useless, and so was his defiance. There was nothing he could do against the thing outside.

Suddenly, crazily, he had a vision of comic-book vampire hunters, going down into Dracula's tomb armed with only a sharpened stick and a cross, driving back the evil monster with nothing but the power of faith, truth and righteousness. That damned animal outside, whatever it was, had hurt him and had hurt his wife. It had tried to drive them against each other. It had laughed at their pain—the pain it had caused! Norman's anger returned, flooding the emptiness the creature had carved in him. Stuffing a handful of shells into the pocket of his flannel pajama shirt, he threw the bolt and kicked open the door. He would not let it win.

Norman didn't need to shout out a challenge. The huge cat stood 40 feet away on the muddy dirt path to the beach, staring at him with the cruel glowing eyes he'd seen in his nightmares. Its dark, snarling pulses of hatred and mockery chilled his soul even as he raised his rifle and screamed.

"Leave us alone!"

The shot cracked sharply in the night. The creature leaped straight up, snarling and twisting in midair. It landed to face Norman once again, fixing him with its horrible glowing green gaze. It opened its mouthful of wicked fangs to unleash an almost-human yowl, and Norman shouted back.

"Get out of here!"

He fired a second shot. Again, the huge beast writhed in the air. When it landed this time, though, it leaped away into the forest with a final, bloodcurdling howl of defeated rage.

Norman pumped shot after frenzied shot into the darkness, loading and firing as fast as his shaking hands could work the bolt. When the last bullet was expended he stood there, panting and trembling, alone in the night. He staggered back into the house, as if in a trance, and dragged himself up the stairs into bed to find Michelle, amazingly, asleep. Even more amazingly, he joined her almost immediately.

Norman woke to sunlight streaming into the cabin and the sounds of singing birds. Birds! It suddenly struck him that during the entire time they'd been out there, they hadn't heard a single bird. It was as if they had been driven away.

He got out of bed and padded to the railing of the loft, looking out the big front window over the mirror-calm lake. He felt a million pounds lighter, almost like he was floating. As he looked around his bright, cheery dream house, he once again saw life in the warm wood, saw a future's worth of memories waiting to be created. Behind him, Michelle rustled the sheets and mumbled contentedly in her sleep.

Behind her, leaning against the cabin's sloping walls, Norman saw the old .22. Someday, he knew, that little rifle would belong to his son.

5
Pranks Gone Bad

The Dog Girl

One night near Halloween, Mitch Smith and his buddies headed into the wooded hills around Cedar Hills, Texas. They had perfect conditions for a spirited game of nocturnal tag: the moonlit night was clear and cool, but not cold, and the light wind made a suitably spooky sound through the trees. Unfortunately, the conditions also happened to be perfect for a terrifying brush with the supernatural.

Now, these boys don't play the schoolyard version of tag. Nocturnal tag is the kind of game you'd expect from a bunch of bored guys with energy to spare and a healthy lack of common sense. "You play it in the woods after dark." Mitch explains. "It starts out like regular tag. One guy gets designated as 'It' and everyone else scatters and hides. The macho bit comes with the tagging. 'It' carries a crossbow, loaded with bolts tipped with padded bags about the size of a silver dollar."

"Well, since it was so close to Halloween, Jason, Mark, Bruce and I decided to play our version of tag out at Mount Lebanon, an area known for occult activity. It's mostly rumor and legend, but a few strange things have occurred there. We stayed outside the boundaries of Mount Lebanon—there's a Christian retreat up there, of all things—and ended up in a wooded area east of the property line. We parked Bruce's yellow Monte Carlo by a big incinerator and headed into the woods. Bruce volunteered to be 'It.' He just enjoyed shooting us, I think."

Mitch and his fellow moving targets scattered widely through the dark autumn woods, hearts pumping and senses heightened. "You get that tingly 'someone is hunting me' feeling," says Mitch. "You sit there waiting to hear the snap of a twig or the twang of a bowstring, waiting to feel the WHAP of one of those damn bolts popping you. The only way to keep from getting shot is to become 'It.' You do this by getting all the way to him and tagging him before he can shoot you. So, generally, you listen to hear the crossbow string pop, then dash like mad to try and tag him before he can reload.

"Well, I was out in the woods, waiting, when I heard a tick-tick-tick...FWOOSH!! sound. It sounded for all the world like a gas stove lighting up—a big gas stove. I remembered the incinerator and figured it must be on a timer...at least, I wanted it to be on a timer." The pleasant thrill of the stalk-and-chase began to slip away fast. A feeling of genuine dread washed over Mitch, filling the dark, dry autumn woods around him.

"I kept thinking, *Someone other than Bruce is watching me.* I began to feel that a bolt in the chest might be worth the risk. If I stepped out of the woods Bruce would shoot me for sure, but if I stayed where I was the non-Bruce—whoever lit that incinerator, my brain kept yammering at me—might do worse.

Mitch wasn't alone in his fear. Just as he was about to emerge from cover and call the game off, he heard Bruce speak out from near the car.

"Bruce was calling us in a sort of higher, trying-not-to-sound-scared voice, saying that maybe we should leave. Mark and I came out of the woods about the same time, and we headed for the Monte Carlo. The incinerator had been turned on, and Bruce swore that he didn't do it. We believed him, because it had a padlocked switch. Now the padlock was gone, and the panel was wide open. We managed to convince each other that someone who worked there must have sneaked past a hyped-up and armed Bruce, silently opened the panel and unlocked the switch, turned the incinerator on, then sneaked back down the open road. Sounded reasonable to us!"

The rationalizations, however far-fetched, comforted the guys for about five seconds—until they realized they were a man short. "All this time," recalls Mitch, "Jason was missing."

"Then, we heard the howling."

It wasn't the distant, comforting sound of Texas coyotes. This was a pack of big dogs in full chase, closing in on the car. In their small clearing, surrounded by suddenly unfriendly trees, the three young men went rigid with fear. Suddenly, their missing friend exploded out of the darkness, white-faced and screaming.

"He was at a dead run," recalls Mitch, "yelling at us to get in the damn car NOW! We didn't stop to ask questions. Mark and I dove into the back seat, and Bruce jumped into the front, flipping madly through his key ring. Jason was about 20 yards or so from the car, and behind him, running out from the tree line, we saw a young girl, obviously terrified.

"Several huge black dogs pursued her into the clearing, their teeth bared. Their howling had degraded into snarling and barking. Jason dove into the car and immediately tried to slam the door shut, but Mark blocked it with his foot, kicking it halfway open. The girl was screaming at us to please help her.

"Jason was screaming, 'Trust me! Let me shut the damned door!' Bruce was whimpering, trying to stab his steering column to death with the ignition key. I sat frozen in the back seat, staring at the dogs and this little girl through the heat haze coming out of the front of the incinerator."

Jason, desperate to seal off the car, cracked Mark across the shin and managed to wrench the door closed, just as the little girl slammed into the side of the car, pleading to be let in. "She looked so scared," says Mitch, "her blonde hair all around her face, obscuring her features.

"The dogs kept charging at a full run—I was sure that I was about to watch them tear the girl apart like a stuffed animal—when they suddenly stopped. The little girl quit pounding on the car door, and calmly stepped back. The dogs all sat down at the same time, like they were at a dog show or something." As the girl stood silently regarding them, the boys felt their stark, mindless panic instantly switch to cold dread.

"I remember most of all the very adult smile that crept across her face as she locked eyes with Jason," Mitch recalls, "like a woman playing coyly with a prospective lover. It was a sickening thing to see on the face of a child—or at least a childlike thing. I have no idea what would have happened if Mark had kept that door open, or if Bruce hadn't managed to start that big damn canary yellow car and tear down that road."

Mitch remembers taking one last look through the rear window. "I can still see that girl and her dogs, fading away in a cloud of dust from the wheels of Bruce's car."

Demon Dogs of the Party Place

Every town has one: the clearing in the woods, the out-of-the-way hilltop or the half-forgotten campsite, where high-school kids go to drink bootlegged beer and party. Legends and lore build up around these spots. Stories of amazing pranks and hilarious misadventures get passed down from graduating class to graduating class, getting more epic with each telling. Some of these take the form of macabre "true stories"—about wandering ghosts, escaped psychopaths, ritual murders and the ever-popular satanic cults—designed to spook one's buddies and make the girls cuddle a little closer.

Roger Healy and his pals in Whitby, Ontario, liked to party at a clearing in the woods north of the nearby town of Ajax. Lying a little east of Salem Road, the party spot inevitably acquired the name "Salem's Lot" (after one of Stephen King's scariest novels). It came equipped with the full complement of dark legends, of black masses, blood-drinking, witches' covens and assorted mayhem. "I thought these stories were just made up to scare the girls," Roger says, "until one night three years ago."

One slow afternoon several years after graduation, Roger had been in a storytelling mood. "I had been telling my friend Jay about all the old high-school legends," he recalls. "I had just gotten my own car, an old '77 Malibu, so we decided to see if we could find the old party spot.

"We drove up to the place where the old road used to take us to the spot, only to find it…gone." It had been five or six years since Roger had been out there, and he knew how quickly weather and weeds can reclaim a neglected road. The pair decided to make a best guess, park the car and hike in.

Roger continues, "As we got further into the woods, we found a path that led between two trees with arcane symbols painted on them. We followed the path through the trees and kept walking until we came to the old dam that I remembered from my high school days. The path had a fork in it, one leading over the dam, and the other leading northwest."

Roger and Jay had not entered the woods totally unprepared. Before setting out into the trees they had looted the miscellaneous junk from the trunk and back seat of Roger's Malibu. In hindsight, this seemingly random collection of tools seems eerily appropriate: a double-edged dagger, a large can of barbecue starter fluid and a dog-eared old copy of the infamous pseudo-diabolical hoax known as the *Necronomicon*—"not that I believe the *Necronomicon* is real, but we had it just the same."

The paperback, a fabrication named after the "book of evil" in H.P. Lovecraft's classic horror novels, put Jay in the mood to play a prank of his own. Jay figured that local "Goth" kids must have painted the trees that gated the path, and he had the perfect scheme to outdo them. "He got this idea to carve a symbol from the Necronomicon into the ground, to scare the pants off of those kids," says Roger. "He has a strange sense of humor."

After a few seconds of leafing through the yellowing pages, the two buddies settled on the template for their goth-frightening masterpiece. They chose the symbol for the demon Pazuzu (the same demon that was supposed to have possessed Linda Blair in the film *The Exorcist*). They pulled out their knife and began gouging the weird looping lines into the weedy topsoil.

They soon made a strange discovery. "Someone had poured asphalt and then buried it under an inch and a half of soil," recalls Roger. "We wondered, *Who would go to all that trouble?*" The old stories of satanic cults instantly sprang to mind. "Yeah, we thought, there must be a body under there! We lit two fires on either side of the hole so we could see what we were doing and started digging. The asphalt came up quite easily, but work was slow as we only had our hands and the knife."

The woods became shrouded in ever-deepening shadow, but Roger and Jay didn't want to stop digging. They felt they were on the verge of uncovering some gruesome ritual murder. Roger suggested heading back to his house for shovels and a flashlight. Before leaving, they picked up handfuls of dirt to smother their two little fires. That's when their nightmare began.

"As we extinguished the last bit of fire," says Roger, "we heard a large dog barking. At first, it sounded like it came from about a mile away, from across a large cornfield that runs parallel to the path. The rows of corn also run parallel to the path."

Something about this sound made the small hairs on the back of their necks stand on end. Unexpected noises on a dark night might spook anyone, but Roger insists that this was more than the barking of an innocent country dog.

"Within about 15 seconds, it grew into the sound of a pack of dogs, tearing something apart that just refused to die. And it kept getting closer. It sounded like it was 50 feet away and coming at us through the cornfield."

Suddenly, a new, even more frightening sound rose in the air. "Above all the howling, screaming and snarling, we heard a high-pitched vibrating whine, not unlike the sound a loose fanbelt makes on a cold winter day. It sent shivers down our spines.

"By now it was about 15 feet from us, and the squeal was deafening." At this point, the would-be cult pranksters lost their nerve. "Jay and I bolted down the path in a complete panic, tripping and falling over branches and undergrowth in the dark. Jay is about six foot one and 180 pounds, and I'm six eight and 220, so normally we aren't scared of anything, but that night we ran like the hounds of hell were after us.

When they reached the old Malibu, the noise stopped. They wrenched the doors open and scrambled into their seats, only to discover that the car's lights, radio and ignition were completely dead—a common occurrence in paranormal experiences. After a terrifying minute of key twisting and button stabbing, the power returned. They floored it out of there.

"To this day, I have no idea what caused that noise," says Roger, "but if we stuck around I wouldn't be here to tell the tale. I have heard wolves, coyotes and bears, but this was like nothing I've heard before."

And what of the mysterious asphalt that supposedly covered some evil cult's unspeakable crime? Roger explains, "After we had some time to calm down, we realized that it was nothing more than the remains of the old road we used to drive down. But I have no idea who made the great effort to ensure it would never be driven down again."

The Screaming Cat

"This mask sucks," said Kevin, pulling off the rubber novelty-store "old man" face. "It's too hot, and I'm gonna have a million zits."

"You idiot," his friend Jack replied, adjusting his own polyester skeleton costume. "Why have you been wearing it this whole time? Not like you could fit any more zits on your face, anyway."

"Shut up!"

"You shut up!"

The two 14 year olds stood whispering in their hiding place—back-to-back closets with a hole punched in the dividing wall so they could talk. The campfire smell of the building's charred timbers surrounded them as they waited for the victims of their prank to arrive.

Earlier that afternoon, on a beautiful late-August day in 1986, Kevin, Jack and their friend Reese had stumbled across the derelict old farmhouse on the city limits. Sometime in the previous few months it had caught fire— or been set on fire—but a brigade from the nearby army base had kept it from burning right to the ground. They left it blackened, waterlogged, sagging and stinking, but still standing. Probably dangerous, too—the kind of place that attracts teenage boys like honey attracts flies.

The old house was already pretty creepy when the boys first checked it out. Grimy light shone dimly through filthy panes of half-smashed glass, illuminating the stained walls and reeking floors. Here and there the boys found the forgotten leavings of the original occupants and more recent guests—random kitchen utensils, a few sticks of wrecked furniture, some broken and half-burnt toys, along with beer cans, cigarette butts and crude graffiti.

Jack came up with the idea for an elaborate prank, and decided the squalid house wasn't quite scary enough for the purpose. "Let's do it up like satanists have been using this place for their rituals," he said. "Then we'll get Brian and Faisal to come out here and we'll scare the crap out of them."

What better way for a bunch of bored brats to spend a long end-of-summer afternoon? After a quick bicycle sprint to the nearby mall, the junior special-effects squad returned to the house armed with clearance-priced costumes and black quick-dry spray paint, ready to create their modest masterpiece of horror.

Their opening scare tactic was an easy bit of cheap shock, more creepy and disturbing than truly scary. They found a dirty and mildewed baby doll, slightly singed and sooty, and hung it by its neck in the front hallway. Its painted plastic stare would provide the perfect teaser for the main set piece in the upstairs bedroom.

Here the boys concocted their "satanic altar," an adolescent vision of evil cobbled together from B-grade horror flicks, heavy-metal album covers and Dungeons & Dragons manuals. They painted a huge black pentagram on the floor and another covering most of one wall. Everywhere else, they scrawled made-up "diabolical" symbols. A battered old stainless-steel salad bowl, containing the remnants and ashes of "burnt offerings," sat in front of the "black altar."

On the altar itself—the dreaded, hellish milk crate—sat the prank's wonderful centerpiece: a genuine cat skull, found in the field on the way back from the mall. Everyone knows no evil satanic altar would be complete without at least one skull. Thanks to their lucky find of the feline head bone, the three frightmasters wouldn't have to resort to the inferior vinyl skull-shaped candle-holder they'd picked up at the novelty shop.

"That skull is awesome," whistled Reese as the trio stood and surveyed their macabre handiwork. "It makes the whole setup." Jack and Kevin agreed that it was indeed totally rad. While Reese rode back to the neighborhood to round up their victims, Jack and Kevin donned their costumes and settled in to wait.

"Shh. Shhh! Here they come," Kevin hissed as the approaching sound of bicycles and voices drifted up from the overgrown yard. Pulling their rubber masks back on, the pair silently listened as Reese brought their unsuspecting buddies into the mouldering old house.

Reese, fairly acknowledged as the champion B.S. artist of their group, was in top form that evening. In hushed and heavy tones, he spun a story of how his "cousin in university" heard that satanists used this place for black rituals. He embroidered the tale with girls going missing, unspecified "sacrifices" and anything else he thought would build atmosphere.

It seemed to work. Brian and Faisal, like many teenage boys, communicated mostly through profanity, so most of their reactions can't be printed. But Brian, normally a loudmouthed and adventurous kid, could barely keep his voice from cracking when he came

across the hanging dolly in the front hall: "Oh, man…
that's just sick."

"Yeah, that's a warning to keep trespassers away," said
Reese. "The satanists don't want anyone to go upstairs. It's
against the satanic bible for any outsiders to see the sacri-
ficial altar."

Upstairs, Jack and Kevin could barely keep from laughing out loud. Reese was outdoing himself this time. Faisal
was fully freaked out: "I…I don't know, guys. Maybe we
should get out of here."

"Don't worry, man…the cult only meets here during
the full moon and the new moon. I think. We'll be out
before sunset, anyway."

"No. No way, forget it. I'm going back outside."

"Fine. Whatever, man. Brian, you coming up or what?"

"Yeah…yeah, let's go." Four feet came clomping up the
old, narrow staircase. Jack and Kevin were almost beside
themselves, waiting for the moment to spring into action.

Brian and Reese stepped into the room, and the two
hidden pranksters heard their unsuspecting buddy swear
under his breath. "Oh, man. Oh, man. Oh, holy…this is
totally freaky."

Reese had dropped his voice to a suspenseful whisper
now, like a golf commentator. "Cool, huh? At first I wondered why there were no bloodstains and stuff. But then I
thought, like, they don't want to waste any, eh? All that's
left is that skull."

"Whoa, yeah…yeah, I guess you're right." The heavy
tread of Brian's hiking boots came farther into the room
as he checked out the "evil" scene. Jack heard him coming
closer and closer to the closet door. It was almost too perfect.

With the clatter of the old brass knob and the creak of a hinge, the door opened. Jack, in skull mask and black skeleton bodysuit, slowly and silently toppled towards Brian, arms extended.

His friend reacted, as Jack recalls, "like Bugs Bunny." Terrified beyond reason, eyes like saucers, he leaped explosively backward, turned in midair and bolted for the door…only to find a screaming old man with wild white hair blocking his path of escape. While Brian had been in the "satanic chapel" Kevin had crept around from the other room. Letting out a wordless half-scream, half-moan, Brian blew straight through Kevin and dove down the stairs in one desperate jump.

"Go, go, go, go, go, GO, GO!" he screamed as he bolted out to his bike. Faisal already sat on his bike, ready for a fast getaway. The pair set a two-wheeled speed record back to town, without a glance back at the brooding, over-grown hell-house they'd barely escaped.

Meanwhile, the maestros of terror killed themselves laughing in their pentagram-covered set.

"Did you see his face? I thought he was gonna wet his pants!"

"He ran right over me, man. Hope he didn't break his arm diving down the stairs."

"Nice work, men," said Reese in his most broad and businesslike manner. "This calls for a little celebration!" With a flourish, he pulled out a six-pack of beer, secretly swiped from his dad's packed fridge—his father's buddies wouldn't miss a half-dozen brewskis, would they?

"Awesome!" They cracked the alcoholic contraband open and passed it around, lounging nonchalantly and pretending to savor the unfamiliar bitter beverage. They'd all tasted beer before, of course, but it was still more an illicit prop than anything. Before long, they had lapsed into typical teenage "drunkenness"—half genuine intoxication and half self-conscious playacting.

"Dude, you were amazing," said Jack, giving Reese a little salute and taking a swig of lager. "That stuff about the full moon, and not wasting any blood? Wicked." He reached out and scratched the cat skull under the chin. "Who's a good kitty, huh? Who's a good little kitty?"

"Thanks, dude. I swear, that idiot Brian would believe…Hey! Shh! Did you guys hear something?" Reese tilted his head, listening.

"Yeah, whatever. Don't try to pull that one on me." Jack laughed and tossed his empty beer can into the hall, where it clattered noisily down the stairs.

"No, seriously, shut up. Listen." Still thinking their friend was just trying to freak them out, Kevin and Jack nonetheless kept still. In the oppressive silence, they became suddenly aware that the sun was going down.

"There! There, you hear that?" They had indeed heard it—an intermittent scrabbling and scraping, like claws on wood. There's nothing unusual about animal noises in an abandoned house, but for a trio of boys already filled with spooky ideas, they proved more than a little disturbing.

"It's uh…it's probably a rat or something," Jack suggested in a hushed tone as the scratching continued.

"There are no rats in this part of the country," Kevin whispered. "And that sounds way too big to be a mouse. It sounds like a cat."

"Yeah, but where's it coming from?" asked Reese, glancing around nervously. Indeed, they couldn't pin down the source of the sound. Every time one of the boys figured out its location, it moved—now in the closet, now behind a wall, now under the warped and worn floorboards.

And was it their beer-tinted imaginations, or was the sound getting louder? Not only louder but more adamant, filling the room, surrounding them. The stale, stinking air of the derelict farmhouse grew heavy with a sense of menace.

"It's…it's everywhere," Kevin stammered. The three friends stood back-to-back-to-back at the center of their joke pentagram, which suddenly didn't seem so funny. Unseen claws skittered and scrabbled all around them. "M-maybe we'd better…"

Just then a terrifying, utterly piercing scream split the air. It was unmistakably a cat's scream, though none of them had ever heard a cat make a sound like that before: equal parts pain, rage and fear. It was a cry to turn blood to ice and bones to jelly.

Not that the boys paused to consciously consider the tone of the hideous scream. They were too busy frantically scrambling over each other, rocketing out of the old farmhouse at the same pace Brian had demonstrated earlier. Driven by liquid fear, the terrible scream howling at their backs, they pedaled furiously for home and safety.

Sitting around later in Reese's basement, the boys did their best to regain their composure. Despite their nervous laughter and feeble attempts at rationalization, they shared a certainty that something weird had happened in the ruined old house.

From his perch on the end of the couch, Jack divided his attention between playing Nintendo and patiently explaining the rational, psychological causes for what they'd experienced.

"All I'm saying is, we were already thinking about satanists and ghosts and curses and stuff, and we heard a stray cat, and we just overreacted and freaked out. What's the code for 99 extra lives?"

"Up, up, down, down, left, right, left, right, B, A, start," Kevin replied. "But how come we never saw or heard any cat the entire time we were there?"

"I don't know…maybe Brian woke it up with all his running and screaming. What—do you think there was some sort of eeeeevil caaaat ghooooooost in the room?"

"No, but…I don't know. Shut up. I'm just saying it was just too freaky to be an ordinary cat."

"You shut up, loser. It's your turn, anyway." Jack, more frightened than he let on, desperately wanted to put the whole experience behind him. He didn't realize that the experience was far from over.

After an hour or so of hanging out, the three friends called it a night. Biking quickly back to his place, Jack felt his uneasiness growing rather than fading. The pleasantly cool night felt clammy, the darkness full of unseen threats. *This is stupid*, he thought as he pushed his bike even faster. *I'm letting those guys get to me.*

Home and a warm bed didn't dispel his lingering fear. Sleep didn't come easily that night, and when it did come it came in fits and starts—restless half-sleep filled with nightmares and sudden panics. Every little noise in the house or yard woke him with a start. He began to feel something waiting for him out there in the blackness.

Around three o'clock in the morning, that something made itself known. Out of sheer exhaustion—physical, mental, emotional—Jack had finally fallen into true sleep about an hour earlier. Suddenly, he snapped back to full terrified wakefulness at an all-too-familiar sound: claws scratching at the wall outside.

Jack sat bolt upright in bed, sweating, on the verge of screaming. But the night was quiet. He sat and listened for the scratching to repeat itself, but heard only the soft sound of his father snoring softly from down the hall. Had he dreamed it? He slowly willed himself to relax.

Then it came, the noise he had hoped he'd never hear again. The howling cat's scream, full of rage and pain, sliced through the night. Jack leaped across the room, switching on the ceiling light, his bedside lamp, his little desktop reading light, and the lava lamp on top of his dresser. In a room as bright as he could possibly make it, he listened.

Silence. The scream didn't return, but neither did sleep. Wide-eyed and wary, Jack lay with his Walkman on and waited for the morning.

After his parents left for work, Jack went immediately to the phone. It rang just as he was about to pick up the handset.

"Hello?"

It was Reese, his voice thin and cracking. "Hey, man."

"Hi. Hey, did you…"

"Yeah, I heard it again. So did Kevin; I just got off the phone with him."

A long pause. "Oh. Oh, man. So…what do we do?"

"Well, uh…Kevin thinks it's that cat skull we found. Like, we disturbed its spirit or something. He says we have to bury it back where we got it."

And so, an hour later, Jack found himself back at the old farmhouse, clutching the short straw he'd drawn. As he prepared to reenter the sinister ruin, he took one last look back at the tiny figures of his luckier friends, standing a very generous safe distance away. Then he hefted his skull-retrieval stick (specially selected for its length), took a deep breath and walked slowly through the door.

The actual operation proved almost anticlimactic. No clawing and scratching greeted him, no screams or yowls blasted him, no waves of terror washed over him. He felt only good old-fashioned self-generated fear as he snagged the bleached bone through an eye socket and gingerly lifted it off its blue plastic altar.

Carrying the thing high and away from him on the end of the stick, like an old-fashioned lamplighter, he walked carefully back to his buddies. Silently, he lowered the skull into the freshly dug hole they had prepared, and Reese covered it with dirt. Kevin sheepishly made a little sign of the cross—"It's what they do in movies, right?"—and the three took off as fast as their bikes could carry them.

"And that was that," says Jack, now a professional free-lance writer and photographer. "None of us ever heard the screaming cat again, and we definitely never went back to that house. That whole area is condos now."

Jack still isn't sure what exactly happened to him and his friends that day. "It could have been psychological, some kind of group hysteria," he says. "We all had each other pretty worked up. Then again, who knows? Maybe we really did disturb some cat spirit."

Jack believes he may carry one lingering effect from the encounter. "This is going to sound nuts," he warns, "but not too long after that I started to get into photography and realized that I was…how should I put this? I was really good at noticing cats.

"Like, everywhere I go I always seem to spot cats that everybody else misses. Cats under bushes, in fourth-story windows…Cats are everywhere, watching us all the time, and hardly anybody ever notices."

Jack laughs. "It's probably because I'm always paying attention, looking for good shots, and the whole cat thing is nothing more than a personal fixation. But, for a while, I enjoyed the fantasy that I'd been granted some kind of supernatural sixth cat sense."

"Still," he says, smiling, "it's kind of weird, isn't it?"

6
Pets Return

A Hungry Kitty

Lined with mature trees and nestled against the magnificent North Saskatchewan River valley, the Grandin district is one of the oldest neighborhoods in Edmonton, Alberta. Although condos and high-rise apartments have long since replaced many of the original Edwardian homes, the historic area is still brimming with ghosts—and not all of them are human.

When Violet, a 29-year-old fashion consultant, and her boyfriend first moved into their big brick house on 111th Street, they had heard the kinds of stories that often come with old homes. The previous tenant of the 100-year-old house described freak zones of cold in the kitchen, "white shadows" in the dirt-floor basement and phantom voices upstairs.

The most persistent spiritual presence in the house made itself known to Violet soon after the couple moved in. "I was unpacking books in the front room," she remembers, "when I heard a loud meowing coming from the hall." Violet went to open the door, thinking it was her cat (a sweet-natured tabby named Soldier) wanting to go outside.

"But when I got to the front door," she says, "Soldier was nowhere around. I opened the door, thinking maybe she had somehow gotten out and wanted back in, but she wasn't there, either." Shrugging it off, she returned to her unpacking. A few minutes later she heard the meowing again, and this time she was certain it wasn't her cat.

"Maybe I was more alert after the first meow, I don't know, but the second meow was much more distinct and I knew it wasn't Soldier." The sound, she says, was "deeper, more guttural, like the distorted voice of a cat that's gone deaf. Soldier might have selective hearing, but she's not deaf."

Over the next few weeks, Violet sensed the phantom feline's physical presence as well. Twice, while napping on the couch, she was woken by the feeling of a cat nuzzling her and sucking her hair. Hair-sucking is a behavior common in cats who were weaned too early, but wasn't one of Soldier's habits. As you might expect, the room was always empty when Violet woke up. She was never startled or frightened by her new ghost pet, whose presence feels "warm and comfortable, like a mild-mannered old tomcat."

Soldier doesn't seem to have a problem with her mysterious roommate, though Violet has occasionally seen her play fighting with an invisible sparring partner or staring intently at empty space. Soldier may simply be exhibiting run-of-the-mill feline eccentricity, but how do you explain her behavior at her food dish?

"About a month after we moved in," Violet recalls, "we moved Soldier's dish to a spot near the back door. That night, when I came home from a birthday party, Soldier greeted me at the door with her loudest, most annoying 'feed me now' voice. I thought it was weird that she'd be so hungry, since I'd only been gone about four hours and I'd filled her bowl before I left."

When Violet went to give Soldier another small helping of food, she was surprised at what she saw. "Her bowl

After a tabby's food began disappearing, it became clear that he had an invisible companion—a spirit cat.

was completely full. It wasn't a different brand of food, and Soldier's never been a picky eater, so I thought maybe she didn't like her bowl's new location." Violet moved the dish back to the old spot, but it didn't help. Soldier refused to eat and kept meowing for dinner until Violet threw the old food out and refilled the bowl.

"This happened a few times over the next month," says Violet, "and it was getting kind of annoying. I couldn't figure out what the problem was." She remained puzzled until she mentioned the strange phenomenon to her family. Her mother, a first-generation Japanese-Canadian, instantly saw what was going on.

Violet's mother said, "The spirit cat is eating the food you put down, in the same way spirits take offerings from shrines." Although the food was physically still there, the ghost cat had consumed its essence. Soldier, attuned as all cats are to the spirit world, saw her bowl as empty. Violet's solution was to set out another, smaller bowl of food beside Soldier's as an offering to the spirit cat.

"I was sort of skeptical," Violet says, "but I figured what the heck; it can't hurt. I started putting a teaspoon or so of dry food down in a small clay bowl every time I fed Soldier, and she never again cried for supper while standing beside a full bowl."

Violet still feels and hears the spirit cat now and then, but it's almost like a member of the family—and the cat-food bills are once again under control.

As Violet says, "It's like having two cats for the price of one."

Lucy's Favorite Pillow

"I know most people don't believe animals have spirits but I believe they do," says Chloe Neuman (not her real name). "After all, anything that can feel love and pain like we do must have a soul." Chloe speaks from firsthand experience—her beloved dog, Lucy, hasn't let death take her from her mistress's side.

One cold and damp January night, Chloe was driving along a stretch of highway outside Knoxville, Tennessee. She spotted a small dog, old and obviously pregnant, snuffling her way across the road, heedless of the speeding cars around her.

"Somehow, she made it to the other side of the highway alive," Chloe recalls. "I pulled over and coaxed her to my car with a can of cat food I had on hand." The shy, gentle beagle had no teeth and seemed lethargic from lack of food. Chloe immediately turned the car around and headed straight for the veterinary hospital.

The vet estimated the dog's age at around 12 years, very old to be carrying a litter. Numerous previous pregnancies had left her belly scarred and covered with cysts, and she had lost her teeth, the vet guessed, by trying to chew her way out of a pen. The vet had to surgically remove the puppies, which were already dead. He told Chloe that an old dog that had suffered this much would likely die within two or three months.

"Well, that was four years ago," says Chloe, "and over those four years, Lucy was my best friend." Chloe and her mother lavished the dog with love and attention, and

Lucy soon became lively and affectionate. She showed none of the behavior problems you might expect in a previously mistreated animal. On the contrary, says Chloe, "Lucy had an aura about her that made people and other animals gravitate to her. It was strange, but when I felt sick or depressed, I could hold her and I would feel better. No other pet had this effect on me."

Eventually, though, old age caught up to the spunky little beagle. "Lucy stopped eating a few a weeks ago. My mother and I took her to the vet, and we found she had kidney failure," Chloe recalls. "Nothing could be done for her." Chloe and her mother took Lucy home and tried to make her as comfortable as possible. But Lucy went downhill quickly, forcing Chloe to make a dreaded decision: to have her beloved dog put to sleep. Coming home from that sad appointment, Chloe was so distraught she had to take a mild sleeping pill in order to get even a few hours of rest.

At some point in the night, despite the effect of the sedative, Chloe woke to a familiar sound. "I may have been groggy, but I know what I heard," she says. "There was a loud snoring sound coming from the den, where Lucy's big pillow lay." When she got up to investigate, the pillow was empty.

When she told the story over breakfast the next morning, her mother said that she too had heard Lucy snoring. "Since then, we hear it all the time," says Chloe. "Even four weeks later she's still snoring."

Chloe and her mother left Lucy's favorite pillow where it had always been until one night, when curiosity got the better of them. They moved the big cushion into a storage closet, just to see what would happen. They didn't hear any snoring that night, Chloe reports, but "the next day, when we woke up, the pillow was back and crushed in as though something had been lying on it.

"It must have been Lucy," she says. "She came home, and is still here in spirit. We'll leave that pillow there for her until she decides to move on." In the meantime, at night, Chloe can still hear the contented snores of her best friend, the gentle old dog she rescued on that cold January night.

The Diagnosis

We tend to think of dogs and cats as natural enemies, locked in an eternal chase of barks, hisses and flying fur—with maybe a mouse added to make it a three-way battle. Of course, animal lovers know this doesn't have to be the case. Dogs and cats raised together, or simply properly introduced, can develop relationships ranging from peaceful coexistence to deep affection. For one such pair of inter-species pals, this bond of friendship reached even beyond death.

When Jeanette first brought Mike into her home, she assumed the basset hound pup would be her one and only pet. But the moment her new friend had settled in, the phone rang. It was an acquaintance from work. She recalled Jeanette mentioning, a few months earlier, that she was considering getting a pet. A stray cat had recently given birth on the co-worker's front stairs. Was

Jeanette still looking for a pet and, if so, would she take one of the kittens?

"Having Mike there must have enhanced my mothering instinct," says Jeanette. Also, she had researched basset hounds before choosing Mike and knew that their laid-back nature helped them get along with other animals. She figured, "What the heck. I love animals, and I finally had my own apartment in a building that allowed pets, so why not?" A week later, a tortoiseshell kitten named London joined the family.

After a remarkably brief period of natural wariness, London and Mike became, as Jeanette puts it, "surrogate littermates."

"At first, it was probably just physical attraction," Jeanette jokes. "They were both fresh out of the litter and obviously loved having another warm body to curl up with and a playmate to socialize with. They'd play fight and stuff, but they were always just playing—they really bonded with each other."

The two became a matched set as they grew older, even going for walks together. Walking a dog and cat at the same time might seem like a handful, but Jeanette says London and Mike developed their own pace: a slow one. "Mike was true to his breed, interested in every little scent, and London had the stereotypical cats' curiosity. They'd just ramble around, checking everything out. It'd sometimes take an hour to go around the block. People would always do a double take when they saw me walking them together."

For five happy years, the dog and cat lived together, ate together and, more often than not, slept together. After

London grew out of kittenhood she'd try to act "cool" about it, Jeanette says, but she snuggled up to warm-bodied Mike at every chance. Sadly, though, all good things come to an end. One summer afternoon, as friends hauled Jeanette's old sofa out to their truck, they carelessly left the front door propped open. London, who had never been allowed to wander outside off her harness and leash, wandered out onto the street and was killed by a car.

"Mike and I were both heartbroken," says Jeanette. "It was such a shock, such a fluke, you know? I'd always tried to be so careful, but this one time…It was like it was meant to happen. Destiny or something." For months, Mike wandered dejectedly around the apartment, snuffling for traces of London's fading scent, whining at night, barely eating.

"He seemed so lost and lonely," Jeanette says. "I gave him as much affection and attention as possible, and I know we both took comfort in each other, but he took a long time to even begin to return to his old self. I even thought about getting another kitten—for about five seconds. There's no way you can replace a member of the family like that."

Things gradually normalized, however. Mike and Jeanette settled into their new routines, and their feline friend became simply a treasured memory. Or did she? According to Jeanette, little tortoiseshell London came back at least once, to save the life of her adopted canine sibling.

"About two years after London was killed, I noticed that Mike had developed a hint of a limp in his right rear leg," Jeanette recalls. "It didn't seem really serious, but I'm a bit of a worrier, so I took him to get checked out."

The veterinarian diagnosed mild arthritis, not unusual in a seven-year-old dog. She didn't see any need for painkillers, as the mild joint ache hadn't yet affected Mike's quality of life. She suggested he shave off a few pounds, to relieve the pressure on his joints. Jeanette went home with a bag of doggy diet food and a reassured mind.

She wasn't reassured for long. That night, disturbing, nightmarish visions disturbed her rest—visions featuring the long-gone London.

"I had dreamt about London many times, of course," says Jeanette, "but those were just normal dreams. I'd never had one this vivid. It was like the dreams you get when you have a fever—a demanding and exhausting closed loop, containing a single powerful image.

"I saw London standing with her forepaws resting on Mike, who lay asleep in his basket. She was meowing insistently, almost crying. Her voice terrified me; she never screamed like that when she was alive. She gazed right at me, just crying and crying. I knew she was trying to tell me something, but in the dream space I didn't know what it was."

Jeanette finally woke up, covered in sweat, with tears in her eyes. As soon as she sat up, she understood London's message. "I just sat there in bed, shaking, thinking, Oh my God...Mike has cancer!" The next morning, when the vet arrived to open her office, Jeanette was waiting ouside the door with Mike.

At first the vet tried to calm her down, to reassure her that Mike's problem was almost certainly arthritis. A radiograph would be expensive, and she hated to see distraught pet owners spending money on panicked testing. But Jeanette wouldn't be denied, and the vet booked the test.

Sure enough, the results showed bone cancer—osteosarcoma, one of the most aggressive and lethal canine tumors. Most dogs with osteosarcoma die, precisely because it's so easily misdiagnosed as arthritis or injury. Fortunately, they had caught Mike's case early enough. If they immediately amputated his leg and began chemotherapy, he could beat it.

"I cried like crazy when I signed the forms for the amputation," says Jeanette, "but I knew it was the only way to save Mike's life." After the surgery and a course of chemo, the vet gave Jeanette the good news: no remaining traces of cancer.

Three years later, Mike is a happy, healthy, 10-year-old, three-legged dog. "He got used to being one leg short really quickly," says Jeanette. "Now he gets around just as easily as ever. To be honest, even when he had four legs he'd never have been mistaken for a racing dog. In fact, he's probably faster now than he used to be; I kept him on that low-calorie diet!"

Jeanette believes Mike owes his life to his old friend. "London somehow managed to bring me a message from the other side. If she hadn't corrected the diagnosis, I'm certain we would have missed the cancer until it was too late. She's the best friend a dog ever had."

Simon's Sympathy

Martin walked aimlessly through the January night, shoulders hunched against the constant freezing drizzle. The typical Vancouver winter weather reflected his thoughts and emotions perfectly. He had never felt so low.

"That was for sure the worst night of my life," Martin recalls. "I had barely any money, no real job, virtually no friends and I'd just been dumped by my girlfriend. All I could think was, *Well, that's it. My whole life now officially sucks.* I felt so miserable, so alone, that I barely noticed or cared that I was freezing cold and soaking wet."

Just three years earlier, he had been riding high. A self-taught web designer and graphic artist, Martin moved to Vancouver to grab his share of the millions of Internet dollars that flowed through the city every day. His talent and his contacts quickly scored him a high-paying, challenging job and through work he'd met Laura, fellow hipster geek and the girl of his dreams. While it lasted, Martin lived in a techno-paradise on the Pacific.

Sadly, Martin arrived just a little bit late for the party. Eighteen months after he staked his claim in the dot-com gold rush, the Internet bubble burst. Newly unemployed techies filled the streets, all scrambling to pay their bills. With limited real experience and no educational credentials, Martin made do with an "almost full time" job at a video rental place.

Martin tried to stick it out, moving from his high-rise apartment to a shared walkup off Davie Street. He nurtured a thin, unsteady stream of freelance work designing web sites for punk rock bands and prostitutes. Laura, on the other hand, sought her opportunities elsewhere. Soon after being pink-slipped, she accepted a year-long contract to teach English in Taiwan.

Despite the ocean that separated them, Martin and Laura decided to stay attached during her time in Asia. "We were in love, or at least I though we were in love," says Martin. "I was sure we could make it. I mean, really, what's a year? My aunt and uncle saw each other something like five times in three years when he worked in the Middle East oilfields."

And so, keeping in touch with cheap e-mail and expensive phone calls, Martin waited. Finally, the day arrived for their big reunion.

Martin power-cleaned his apartment, doing his best to transform it into a romantic love-nest, and bribed his musician roommate to stay away for a while. He planned to take Laura directly from the airport to the Gyoza King restaurant on Robson Street, where they had had their first date. It would be perfect.

"Looking back, I put way too much emotional investment into that night," Martin admits. "For a year I had sort of put myself on 'pause.' I kept telling myself, When Laura gets back I'll do blah blah blah. 'When Laura gets back' became this magical date when suddenly everything would be wonderful."

It was not to be. In the cozy warmth of the little restaurant, over a plate of their favorite Japanese dumplings, Laura dropped her bomb. She had met another guy in Taiwan a few months ago, she said. She hadn't told Martin because she wanted to tell him face-to-face. She had only come home for a few weeks to put some affairs in order and renew her visa before returning to her new lover.

"I just snapped," says Martin. "I threw money on the table and ran out of the restaurant. I wandered the streets through the rain, crying, kicking garbage cans and stuff. I had built up all this hope and tension and expectation over the course of a year, and she blew it all away in a couple of seconds." Eventually, drenched to the bone and exhausted, Martin found his way back to his empty apartment.

"It all hit me again when I came home. I saw the wine on the table and the candles ready to be lit. I thought I was cried out but I just dropped down and cried again. Then I broke some things. Then I drank the wine. I was a mess."

Physically and emotionally drained, Martin put on some dry pajamas and crawled into bed, but even with the wine in him he couldn't sleep.

"All I wanted was to sleep, to just shut down and not wake up for a long time, but I couldn't. The same thoughts kept circling my mind, like a fever dream—waves of panic and anger and despair. I tried every sleeping trick I knew—relaxation exercises, counting backwards—but nothing could calm me down."

Then, as Martin lay alone in the dark, his roommate's cat, Simon, jumped onto the end of his bed and walked up his body onto his chest. This struck Martin as very strange, for two reasons. First, the notoriously cranky cat barely tolerated its owner, let alone Martin. Second, Simon had been dead for three weeks.

Martin's eyes snapped open. Even in the dim light, there was no mistaking Simon's blunt, mottled brown muzzle staring him in the face. The supposedly dead cat crouched on his chest, emitting a rumbling purr. Strangely, says Martin, "I didn't freak out at all. I felt a sort of electric tingle, goosebumps, all over my body, but there was no fear.

"In fact, it was the opposite. As soon as the initial shock wore off, I felt this wave of warmth and comfort, of sympathy. Simon just purred and curled up on top of me, looking me in the eyes.

"All my racing crazy thoughts melted away. I was still heartbroken, but my sadness had become calmer, something I could cope with." Martin reached up and petted his eerie visitor—"I could feel his fur and his warm body under my hands"—and fell asleep to his purring.

"The next morning, I woke up totally refreshed," says Martin. "It was weird, like I'd had some sort of enlightenment. I still had all these negative emotions, but they were, I don't know, more productive? I just felt confident I could deal with the Laura thing, and with my crappy life." Martin even rediscovered his sense of humor. "I actually said out loud to myself, 'Well, at least you got a clean apartment out of the deal.' "

When his roommate returned home later that morning, Martin cautiously told him about his face-to-face encounter with Simon. His roommate, a die-hard materialist, offered his own skeptical (but sympathetic) explanation. "He just put his arms around my shoulders," Mike recalls, "and said 'Dude, it was just sleep paralysis.' "

Sleep paralysis often generates elaborate, realistic hallucinations, he said. At times of high stress, people sometimes slip into a state between waking and dreaming, in which the mind is partially conscious but the body remains immobilized by sleep.

The theory seemed to fit, but Martin remained unconvinced. "I've had all kinds of crazy experiences with sleep paralysis," he explains, "but I would never describe them as peaceful or tranquil.

"When you're in that state," he says, "you can't move, you can't speak or scream. You keep slipping back and forth into dreams and weird visions. I've seen the shirts hanging from the back of my door turn into evil robed cultists. I've felt totally convinced that there was a crowd of people in my room, just out of my visual range. It's terrifying."

So, what exactly happened that night? If Simon's ghost really did return, why did he choose to appear to a human that detested him in life? "Maybe that's exactly the point!" Martin exclaims. "That cat never had any use for me, and I never had any use for it—until that night. Maybe he came back because I finally needed him.

"I don't know if it was actually Simon's ghost, or if he was just a hallucination. A dude I know who's into witchraft tried to tell me that the cat was a demon, and he came to 'feed on my pain' or whatever. If that's the case, I say, he can come back any time for seconds.

"I guess I'm saying that it doesn't matter what really happened. All I know is, one minute I was on the verge of an emotional breakdown, the next minute I was snuggling up to a supposedly dead cat, and the next minute everything was cool. I'll never explain it, so I'll just accept it and move on."

Cyrano's Farewell

When Penny first met Cyrano at the animal rescue agency, she saw little hint of the playful, energetic mynah he would one day become. His bedraggled feathers hung dull and matted, and some were even split or frayed. His yellow beak had gone soft from lack of necessary dietary minerals, and his frightened eyes held none of the luster of a healthy bird's. He was, in Penny's words, "a heartbreaking sight…a real mess.

"I almost cried to think that someone could let him get to that state. His previous owners had no clue what was involved in taking care of a mynah, or any exotic bird for that matter. I was told they were feeding him things like peanuts and apple slices.

"I don't think they were malicious or anything—at least, I don't like to think they were," says the vivacious mother of three. "It was just lucky for Cyrano they realized that they were in over their heads and took him to the shelter."

Penny had never owned a bird more exotic than a budgie. She could never have afforded a parrot or mynah from a conventional source. But she had done her reading, and when a friend at the shelter told her about Cyrano she knew she wanted to adopt the forlorn bird.

"He was a real fixer-upper," she jokes. "At first, we had to hand-feed him with a dropper. He hadn't been physically injured or mishandled by his previous owners, thank God, so he wasn't afraid of humans. But his awful diet had made him lethargic and stunted his mental

Did a mynah named Cyrano wait until the afterlife to imitate the sound of an alarm keypad?

development. Once he got some energy back, he went through a phase where he was incredibly moody. I don't know if birds can be manic-depressive, but Cyrano sure came close."

With patience, a proper diet, intellectual stimulation and good old-fashioned TLC, Cyrano eventually regained the mischievous high spirits mynahs are known for.

"Oh, Lord, he was a handful," Penny laughs. "For curiosity, he was worse than any cat. You had to keep an eye on him all the time when he was out of his cage." Apparently, you also had to keep an eye on him when he was in his cage: "The little latch on his door was the first thing he figured out how to operate."

For five years, Cyrano's playful spirit filled the household. He especially loved playing hide and seek. "He was always hiding little things away," laughs Penny. "Even a year after he was gone, when I'd clean the house, I would find his little treasures, barrettes and stuff, hidden in nooks and crannies."

But, like most mynah birds, Cyrano's favorite game involved mimicking sounds around the house.

"He never really tried hard to do human voices or English words," recalls Penny. "He was more a fan of mechanical noises. The beeps of the microwave, the ringing of the phone, that kind of thing. Any time we brought some new noisemaker into the house, you could tell he was intently listening to it. He loved new sounds as much as he loved new trinkets.

"He'd get especially excited whenever the kids got a new Nintendo game," she adds. "He'd watch them play for hours. They just loved it when he first started copying Super Mario, and he ate up the attention. After that, there was no getting away from the sound of Mario going down those pipes."

One day, though, the inevitable happened. "The boys came home from school," Penny recalls, "and they found him lying dead in his cage. He was peppy as ever that morning, and then...poof. Gone.

"He just went," says Penny. "Maybe he'd been living on borrowed time for as long as we'd had him—I don't know. I guess it was just his time."

That evening they buried Cyrano with full honors under a Russian olive tree in the backyard, and the grieving family went to bed in a sadly silent house. "It's weird, you know?" Penny muses. "You never really realize how much you can miss a sound until it's gone. Even when he wasn't squawking, Cyrano was always there in the background, rattling his cage or whatever. The house seemed so quiet with him gone."

For Penny, sleep didn't come easily that night. She tossed and turned restlessly through the hours, never more than half asleep. Then, around three in the morning, a familiar sound from downstairs jolted her awake.

"Our house has an electronic burglar alarm," Penny explains, "and that night, I swear I heard the sound the keypad makes when you set the system before leaving the house: four beeps as you punch in the code, then five really quick beeps that tell you the system's armed."

Puzzled, Penny went downstairs to check it out. She found the alarm just as she'd set it before going to bed, with the doors and windows alarmed and the interior motion sensors bypassed so the family wouldn't set them off if they got up during the night. Thinking she must have been hearing things, Penny headed back upstairs.

"I suddenly realized what I had actually heard," she says. "It had sounded like the burglar alarm being set, but the beeps had a more grating, less electronic tone. I knew then and there that I had heard the sound of Cyrano imitating the sound of the alarm keypad.

"The weird thing is, and I didn't really realize it until that moment, but when Cyrano was alive he never mimicked the sound of the alarm being set. He'd make beeps and stuff, but never that 'beep-beep-beep-beep-bipbip-bipbipbip' sequence."

A flash of insight hit Penny then, one that caused her to sit down on the stairs and weep in a mixture of joy and grief.

"I think Cyrano associated the arming of the alarm with us leaving the house, leaving him alone. It was a lonely sound for him, and that's why he never wanted to copy it. I'm sure he knew that sound—he heard it every day—but for him it meant 'goodbye.'

"I'm sure that's what I heard that night," says Penny, with firm conviction in her voice. "I heard Cyrano saying 'goodbye' to us for the first and last time."

Home from the Road

Many tales of animal phantoms take on epic proportions. The creatures appear amid thunder and lightning, snarl frightening warnings in the night, predict future disaster or bear ghostly witness to ancient tragedies. Even the ghosts of ordinary family pets often take on larger-than-life roles after death. They bark at midnight to wake the household in time to escape an undetected Christmas tree fire, or appear at a bedside to give comfort when it's most needed.

These encounters make for great stories, but animal spirits often manifest themselves in much more subtle ways. They return with the simple but undeniable feeling of their presence.

Al and Lorraine decided to take semi-retirement while they were in their 30s—"still young enough to enjoy it," as Lorraine says. Al, a professional technical writer, left a senior full-time salaried position to become a freelance contractor. Lorraine maintained a home business, handcrafting custom silverwork. They hoped to keep their work time as personal and flexible as possible, to allow them to indulge their true passion: touring America in their cozy camperized van.

They sometimes spent months on these road trips, accompanied by their big orange tomcat Chisholm, named after the legendary cattle trail. Unlike most cats, Chisholm didn't mind spending long periods in a vehicle. In fact, his favorite position in the van—when he wasn't curled up in the back seat, letting the road rock him to sleep—was right up front with his owners, paws on the dash, watching the country roll past their little house-on-wheels.

Beginning when was a kitten, Lorraine and Al had taken Chisholm in the car or van whenever possible, to get him used to it. The early training worked almost too well. Chisholm seemed bored and restless whenever they spent time at home. Like his owners, he got tired of always seeing the same sights and smelling the same scents. He much preferred the road.

For five years Chisholm rode the highways with Al and Lorraine, visiting at least 30 states. He explored the rugged coast of Alaska and the deserts of the Southwest. He saw the mighty Mississippi and the Great Lakes. Then, one fall day in Florida, Chisholm went missing.

The traveling couple, with their tabby navigator, had arrived at their campground outside of Clewiston, on the shores of Lake Okeechobee. Lorraine opened up the van and began unpacking their "living room"—two comfy folding chairs and a rickety old card table.

Normally, their first order of business would be to put Chisholm in his kitty harness and tether. He was asleep, so Lorraine began unloading the gear before leashing him. While she was busy, Chisholm must have followed his curiosity out of the van.

Of course, they panicked when they couldn't find him. They searched for Chisholm frantically until the sun set, canvassing the other campers and literally beating the bushes. A few folks had seen Chisholm, but nobody knew where to find him. The distraught couple heard every solemn theory about what might have happened to their cat, from highway traffic to alligators.

For Al and Lorraine, the disappearance of their cat couldn't suppress the warm spirit his presence created.

As you might expect, they little enjoyed the rest of their holiday. For over a week, they maintained a somber vigil at their campsite. Sitting out under their awning, they played cribbage to pass the time and waited for their cat to come back. Finally, after eight days, the time came to pack up and go home. Leaving Chisholm's picture and vital statistics with the campground managers, the heavy-hearted couple headed home. Their van suddenly felt two sizes too large.

If you've ever lost a beloved pet, you know the hole it leaves in your life. As Al and Lorraine drove home, nothing seemed right anymore. Chisholm had been such a part of who they were. Lorraine alternated between two unbearably painful shades of self-incrimination. She berated herself for letting Chisholm slip out in the first place, and for "abandoning" their orange ball of joy in Florida.

Two weeks after they returned to their unhappy home, things were slowly returning to normal. They had work to do, orders to fill, friends to see and errands to run. They even began to talk about adopting another cat, though they knew Chisholm could never truly be replaced.

That idea soon went right out the window. One night, Al awoke to a familiar sound. Out of reflex, he got out of bed and headed into the hallway. Halfway to the back door, the realization hit him. He had heard Chisholm at the door and was on his way to let him in.

Of course, he knew he must have been dreaming. Even if Chisholm was somehow alive, he was half a continent away. Nevertheless, he still found himself going down the stairs, turning on the yard light and opening the screen door—just in case. As he walked back to bed he tried to tell himself, *I was just checking the yard.* Still, he was glad that Lorraine hadn't seen him "let the cat in."

When he got to the bedroom, though, he found Lorraine sitting up in bed, her eyes wide. "You heard him, didn't you?" she asked, her voice filled with emotion.

"What are you talking about?" said Al. "I thought I heard something in the backyard. Forget about it. It was just a dream."

"No it wasn't, Al," Lorraine declared. "I heard it, too...or felt it. It was Chisholm, and you got up to let him in."

"It was just a weird dream, honey," Al replied, rolling over and making a show of yawning and snuggling into his pillow. "Let's get some sleep, okay?" Of course, neither of them got much sleep that night.

Over the next couple of days, even the adamantly skeptical Al had to admit that something strange was going on. There wasn't any sort of spectacular strangeness—no phantom footprints, no unexplained noises or mysterious topplings of items from shelves—but a familiar feeling had once again filled the house. They could sense that Chisholm was back, sharing a home with his human friends.

They never heard the noise at the back door again. Apparently, once Chisholm had been let back in his spirit happily remained indoors. Al, reading the morning paper, would absentmindedly reach down to scratch a furry head, only to find his fingers twiddling in empty air. Lorraine, taking a bath, would feel curious cat eyes on her. When she looked up, she'd catch a half-glimpse of orange fur darting around the corner. Midnight pillow-side purring, sudden sidesteps as they felt a feline under foot—Chisholm was somehow still in the house, however you care to explain it.

Lorraine believes that Chisholm's spirit found its way back home and is spending time with his family before "passing on." Al takes a more rational approach. Chisholm's "ghost," he maintains, is just a holdover of old habits and expectations. For years Chisholm had played an integral role in their everyday lives, and the suddenness of his departure only enhanced that sensation.

Al believes his theory holds just as much emotional meaning as Lorraine's. "It's a pretty powerful statement on how interconnected humans and animals can be," he says. "The habits of living with a pet have been wired into us so firmly that it feels like there's still a cat in the house. We're reacting on autopilot to something that's not there anymore. It's sort of scary, but that's how humans work."

Lorraine counters with an overlooked bit of data: "If Chisholm's ghost is a product of our imaginations, filling in the blanks left open by our habits, why did it take two weeks for the phenomenon to kick in?" She believes that it took that long for Chisholm's spirit to make its way home, and that Al spiritually let the cat back in when he opened the screen door.

Their debate, though, is merely academic. Neither of them deny that they have experienced something rare and extraordinary. Figment or phantom, the presence of Chisholm inhabits their home. When they pulled away from that Florida campground, they believed that he was gone from their lives forever. Now, they've been given a chance to properly say goodbye to their lost friend.

Even as this is being written, the couple is planning their next road trip—to Canada's East Coast, maybe, or Mexico. They've hung around home long enough, they say, and Chisholm seems to feel the same way. He has been appearing less frequently, and the sense of him in the house has gradually faded. Soon, say Al and Lorraine, it will be time for all of them to take their next journey.

A Message from Moby

Brent Jansen had been having the trip of a lifetime, back-packing with college friends for five weeks through the length and breadth of Ireland. He and his buddies wandered from the weird volcanic formations of the Giant's Causeway in the north to Blarney Castle with its famous stone in the south, from the majestic cliffs of Slieve League in County Donegal to the mysterious ancient tomb of Newgrange in Glendalough. All along the way, they enjoyed Ireland's food, music, people and, of course, pubs. They sat in dozens of pubs and quaffed hundreds of pints, Beamish stout and Harp lager, joining forces with Irish whiskey and "Scrumpy Jack" cider in a happy blur of Celtic joy.

And now, fresh from a pilgrimage to the famous Guinness brewery, Brent lay in his bed at Dublin's cosy Tathony House hostel. Tomorrow, it was back to London and from there the long transatlantic flight home to Calgary. As much as he'd loved Ireland, the young man looked forward to getting back, with his bag full of photos and his head full of stories.

It didn't take long for Brent to fall asleep that night (he had thoroughly sampled the Guinness family's fine products). But he didn't snore peacefully for long. At about two o'clock in the morning he began to dream, a dream more immediate and vivid than any he'd had before: a vision of the death of one of his oldest and dearest friends.

In his dream, he found himself in the familiar surroundings of Calgary's Nose Hill park, a little piece of unspoiled wilderness in the midst of modern housing developments, not far from his parents' home. Brent often spent hours hiking through the park, enjoying the quiet and solitude. The dream sight of its foothills terrain— wild grasses and scrub rustling in the dry summer wind, the evening sun throwing its long shadows—filled him with a mix of happiness and homesickness. But something wasn't quite right. Everything looked familiar but was somehow different. When the dream revealed his pet cat, Moby, loping through the familiar grassland, he realized what he was seeing.

"I was down almost at cat level," Brent remembers, "not seeing through Moby's eyes, but still somehow experiencing what he was experiencing." The big old platinum Siamese was moving unusually fast for his advanced age—over 16 years and counting, with more than a touch of arthritis in his back legs. Brent's parents were cat-sitting; he had left strict instructions for them not to let the aged but feisty tomcat out. Moby was far too rickety to deal with any trouble his temper might get him into.

Brent knew that his dream was actually happening. As the vision continued, the reason for the old cat's painful sprint became clear.

"He was being hunted," says Brent. "There are lots of coyotes in that area, and they take what they can get. They can't usually catch cats, but Moby was a pretty easy target: old, fat and slow." The cat tried to make a run for it, but adrenaline can only make up for so much. Brent could feel Moby's exhaustion, feel the pain in his legs, feel the electric panic of a frightened feline. Worst of all he could feel his childhood pal losing steam, and with the cat's

senses he could hear, smell and even feel the canine predator closing in. Yards behind, feet, inches…

It was all over in an instant. The golden sunshine of a
clear mid-July evening in southern Alberta vanished,
replaced by the close darkness of the Dublin night. Brent
awoke suddenly, disoriented, his heart pounding.

"I knew Moby was dead, and I knew that I had watched
it happen," Brent says. "It was an absolute conviction."

The strange dream left him mystified and disturbed
but, oddly, Brent didn't feel upset by Moby's death itself.
"Maybe it was the certainty of knowing," he speculates,
"that sort of calm that comes when there are no questions
or loose ends. I knew he'd been killed, but I also knew that
he was beyond the reach of pain and suffering. I think it
would have been worse if I had arrived home and he was
just gone."

After the flight home, Brent's parents met him at the
airport. He says, "They didn't waste any time in letting me
know about Moby. After the hugs and kisses, picking up
my luggage and getting on the road home, my mom
turned around in the front seat and looked at me with a
really strange expression. She said, 'Honey, before we get
home, there's something you should know…'

"I just put my hand on her arm and said, 'I know,
Mom. Moby's gone. It's okay.' Her eyes went wide. She just
stared at me, half-stammering, not knowing what to say.
She asked, 'How do you know?' "

Brent told them about the dream he'd had in Dublin,
and his amazed parents confirmed that the times matched
up perfectly. Moby had gotten loose at more or less
exactly the time that Brent had his vision. Brent's mom

had been grilling steaks on the barbecue. She wasn't used to having a cat around the house and had absentmindedly left the patio door open when she went in to answer the phone. The veteran tomcat had siezed the opportunity and literally headed for the hills.

"Mom started to cry a little," Brent continues. "She felt really guilty and embarrassed for letting the cat out. They hadn't stopped searching the neighborhood until they had to leave for the airport to pick me up. I just said 'Don't worry, it's okay. He's gone and it's over. It was his time. There's nothing you could have done.'"

When Brent got back to his parents' place, he went straight out to Nose Hill Park. With no difficulty, he found the exact spot he'd seen in his dream, the spot where Moby died. He couldn't see any blood or bones— "Coyotes are pretty thorough," he says—but he sat there for a long time, meditating and reflecting on his seemingly supernatural experience.

Brent still visits that spot often. He sits amid the wild beauty of the Rocky Mountain foothills and thinks about the day his old friend somehow reached across half a planet for one last moment of connection.

Delilah

When Tracy Rybak first met Delilah, the wary Rottweiler was incarcerated on the Vancouver animal shelter's "Death Row"—slated to put to sleep, unwanted and allegedly vicious. But Tracy didn't see an out-of-control beast; she saw a frightened dog who'd been raised wrong and treated poorly, waiting for some human to give her love, care and a happy life. The moment she met Delilah, Tracy decided that she would be that human.

"They said she was vicious with animals and small children," Tracy recalls, "although the entire time she was with me she was never mean to any small animal, or to a small kid."

And who knows? Maybe Delilah's alleged ferocity was a factor, conscious or not, in Tracy's decision to bring her home. As a young woman living alone on an isolated acreage outside Whitecourt, Alberta, part of Tracy's desire to own a dog came from a need for a sense of protection and security. What better rural security system than an overprotective Rottweiler that doesn't take kindly to strangers?

Tracy's father, who lived in Maple Ridge, British Columbia, drove his daughter and her new companion home to Alberta, a long ride through the breathtaking terrain of the B.C. Interior and the Rocky Mountains. The only problem was there wasn't room in the cab of the truck for two adults and a big, nervous dog, and Tracy refused to leave Delilah alone in the cargo bed. There was only one solution.

"I had her in the back of the truck and I rode all the way home with her," Tracy remembers. "Thirteen hours in the back of a truck. It gave me a chance to bond with her."

It was a noisy and bumpy ride, but Tracy made Delilah and herself as comfortable as could be expected with a nest of pillows and blankets. Delilah, newly sprung from a small cage in a room full of other frightened animals, was initially nervous on the road, but one of the great abilities of dogs is to recognize when they're loved.

"It was an experience," says Tracy. "She was really reserved at first, you know, and then she got to know me." By the time her dad's truck crunched its way up the gravel driveway, Tracy and Delilah were fast friends.

Nurtured for possibly the first time in her life, Delilah took instantly to her role as companion and protector, jealously guarding her mistress and their property with unwavering vigilance.

"She was a good guard dog," says Tracy, smiling. "She would never let anybody out of their vehicle if they came, until I said it was OK.

"She was great for Jehovah's Witnesses, too," Tracy says with a laugh. Their unwanted visits gave Delilah a chance to showcase her acting abilities. "I would just go to the door and hold her as if it was taking all my strength to keep her back," says Tracy. "She'd lean against me, really straining against the leash, and just growl, and they'd leave quickly."

For over three years, Delilah guarded the acreage and kept her mistress company. Eventually, Tracy began a promising romance with Ron, a local RCMP officer. Things progressed well, and eventually it was time for

Tracy's new boyfriend to come out to the property and be introduced to Delilah.

"That day, the first day I ever brought him over to my house, I was really excited for him to meet my dog," Tracy remembers. "She was always a really good judge of character, so I was anxious to see what she thought of him, you know? Kind of like the ultimate character test.

"We got home," Tracy continues, "but she wasn't there." Tracy and her friend had a quick look around and then went inside for coffee. Tracy tried to reassure herself that Delilah had just wandered off following some scent or another, that she'd come trotting back at any moment, but still she was uneasy and distracted as she and Ron chatted in her kitchen.

"After we'd had coffee and he'd gone home, I went looking for Delilah in earnest," she says. "I never, ever found her."

Tracy knew that Delilah, whose loyalty was unwavering, would never just wander off for any length of time. She didn't even like to go out of sight of the house. She had no proof, but in her heart she knew with near certainty what had become of her dog.

"I think what happened is that the neighbor shot her. He was a real foul old man...someone you just didn't want around." According to Tracy, the neighboring farmer had a long-standing beef with the vigilant Delilah.

"He'd go out to his hay field right next door, and sometimes she would follow him around on his tractor all day," Tracy explains. "Whenever he wanted to get out of the tractor, she wouldn't let him. She was kind of protective of the property."

That day, Tracy thinks, the sour old farmer, out of meanness or drunkenness or both, decided to take care of his problem in the bluntest, most brutal manner. "I think that's what happened to her, anyway," she says, sighing. "I couldn't prove it, though. She was just gone."

When she got to missing her faithful Rottweiler too much, Tracy would console herself with a different theory: "I was dating a cop, so I thought maybe she knew I didn't need her protection anymore, and she went to look after somebody else." It was a nice thought, that the ever-vigilant Delilah was somewhere out there, keeping somebody safe. It wasn't long before Tracy had an experience that, for her, turned that fantasy into fact.

"It was several months later," Tracy begins, "and the relationship had progressed between me and Rob." It had the potential to be a really good thing, but differences in their lifestyles were threatening to scuttle the romance before it had a chance to bloom.

"He was a cop and I was a bartender," Tracy says, "and that was starting to become a conflict of interest. I'd get him drunk and he'd give me an impaired [driving charge]. So that was getting to be a problem."

It wasn't the only problem. The clash of lifestyles between a law-and-order Mountie and a hard-partying small-town girl went deeper and darker. "I would occasionally do drugs," Tracy admits, without volunteering any details, "and that was a conflict in our relationship as well."

Eventually, inevitably, these conflicts all came to a head. "We got into a big argument," Tracy explains. There was shouting, accusations, hurtful things said.

Finally, hours later, Rob had to go on duty, leaving the argument hanging.

"He had driven me back and dropped me off at his house. I went to bed thinking about whether to give him up or give up the lifestyle that I was used to." The distraught young woman lay awake in Rob's bed, alternating between rage at him for forcing her into making a choice and despair at the thought of losing him.

"All of a sudden there was a light in the hallway," she says, "and there was a shadow on the wall. I looked and then there was the dog." It was her old friend and protector, Delilah, padding softly into the dim bedroom.

"She came into the room and she jumped on the bed. She lay down beside me, and I could feel her weight."

It was that physical feeling, the sense of her beloved guard dog on the bed with her, that has Tracy convinced that Delilah's appearance was no creation of a desperate and fearful psyche. "It was so real," she says. "I could feel the weight of her lying beside me.

"She just lay down beside me, and then I fell asleep. I had stopped worrying about everything. And when I woke up, she was gone."

Delilah's return had taken away more than Tracy's panicked worry. "That's when I quit drugs forever," says Tracy with firm finality. "That was nine years ago."

Tracy wasn't frightened during the ghostly experience. "I wasn't scared. It was cool because I thought 'Oh, OK...you are somewhere,' you know? I'd wondered where she went, and wherever it was it was a good place. She came back just to let me know she was still watching over me. Like a guardian angel."

Enjoy more terrifying tales in these collections by

GHOST HOUSE BOOKS

THE CHILLS AND THRILLS JUST KEEP COMING AT GHOST HOUSE BOOKS! BE SURE TO ADD THESE NEW TITLES TO YOUR COLLECTION.

Romantic Ghost Stories *by Julie Burtinshaw*
Love conquers everything, as a poet once wrote, but can it survive death? This new collection, based on true accounts, explores lovers united in death, the lasting effects of a lost love among the living and, most dramatically, the tempestuous infidelities whose painful conse-quences never fade away.
$10.95USD/$14.95CDN • ISBN 1-894877-28-4 • 5.25" x 8.25" • 224 pages

NEW MAY 2004 • **Urban Legends** *by A.S. Mott*
This entertaining volume collects and explains many of the modern myths that do the rounds at water coolers across the nation. If you've ever wondered about the notorious vanishing hitchhiker or the story about the rodent that turns up in a bucket of fried chicken, this book will prove essential reading.
$10.95USD/$14.95CDN • ISBN 1-894877-41-1 • 5.25" x 8.25" • 216 pages

NEW JULY 2004 • **Haunted Cemeteries** *by Edrick Thay*
Cemeteries are places of quiet repose where the dead are left to their eternal rest. But some spirits just can't sleep. In this new collection, Edrick Thay shares eyewitness accounts set in graveyards around the world, including the notorious Bachelor's Grove in Chicago, the vampire-plagued Highgate Cemetery in London and the ancient Valley of the Kings in Egypt.
$10.95USD/$14.95CDN • ISBN 1-894877-60-8 • 5.25" x 8.25" • 216 pages

NEW AUGUST 2004 • **Werewolves and Shapeshifters** *by Darren Zenko*
Werewolves and shapeshifters are fascinating beings, capable of shifting from ordinary to extraordinary in the blink of an eye. Join Darren Zenko as he narrates fictionalized accounts of the werewolf and shapeshifter lore from around the globe.
$10.95USD/$14.95CDN • ISBN 1-894877-53-5 • 5.25" x 8.25" • 232 pages

These and many more Ghost House books are available from your local bookseller or by ordering direct. U.S. readers call 1-800-518-3541.
In Canada, call 1-800-661-9017.